Bible Romances

G. W. Foote

Bible Romances
Copyright © 2020 Bibliotech Press
All rights reserved

The present edition is a reproduction of previous publication of this classic work. Minor typographical errors may have been corrected without note, however, for an authentic reading experience the spelling, punctuation, and capitalization have been retained from the original text.

ISBN: 978-1-64799-368-9

CONTENTS

THE CREATION STORY 1
NOAH'S FLOOD 12
EVE AND THE APPLE 23
THE BIBLE DEVIL 34
THE TEN PLAGUES 45
JONAH AND THE WHALE 56
THE WANDERING JEWS 67
THE TOWER OF BABEL 78
BALAAM'S ASS 89
GOD'S THIEVES IN CANAAN 100
CAIN AND ABEL 111
LOT'S WIFE 121

THE CREATION STORY

The Book of Genesis is generally thought, as Professor Huxley says, to contain the beginning and the end of sound science. The mythology of the Jews is held to be a divine revelation of the early history of man, and of the cosmic changes preparatory to his creation. The masses of the people in every Christian country are taught in their childhood that God created the universe, including this earth with all its flora and fauna, in five days; that he created man, "the bright consummate flower" of his work, on the sixth day, and rested on the seventh. Yet every student knows this conception to be utterly false; every man of science rejects it as absurd; and even the clergy themselves mostly disbelieve it Why, then, do they not disabuse the popular mind, and preach what they deem true instead of what they know to be false? The answer is very simple. Because they feel that the doctrine of the Fall is bound up with the Genesaic account of Creation, and that if the latter be discredited the former will not long be retained. The doctrine of the Fall being the foundation of the scheme of Atonement, the clergy will never admit the Creation Story to be mythical until they are forced to do so by external pressure. At any rate they cannot be expected to proclaim its falsity, since by so doing they would destroy the main prop of their power. What the recognised teachers of religion will not do, however, should not be left undone, especially when it is so needful and important. Men of science, by teaching positive and indisputable truths, are gradually but surely revolutionising the world of thought, and dethroning the priesthoods of mystery and superstition. Yet their influence on the masses is indirect, and they do not often trouble themselves to show the contradiction between their discoveries and what is preached from the pulpit. Perhaps they are right. But it is also right that others should appeal to the people in the name not only of science, but also of scholarship and common sense, and show them the incredible absurdity of much that the clergy are handsomely paid to preach as the veritable and infallible Word of God.

The Creation Story, with which the Book of Genesis opens, is incoherent, discrepant, and intrinsically absurd, as we shall attempt to show. It is also discordant with the plainest truths of Science. Let us examine it, after casting aside all prejudice and predilection.

If the universe, including this earth and its principal inhabitant, man, was created in six days, it follows that less than six thousand years ago chaos reigned throughout nature. This, however, is clearly untrue. Our earth has revolved round its central sun for numberless millions of years. Geology proves also that million years have elapsed since organic existence first appeared on the earth's surface, and this world became the theatre of life and death. Darwin speaks of the known history of the world as "of a length quite incomprehensible by us," yet even that he affirms "will hereafter be recognised as a mere fragment of time" com-pared with the vast periods which Biology will demand. The instructed members of the Church have long recognised these-statements as substantially true, and they have tried to reconcile them with Scripture by assuming that the word which in the History of Creation is rendered day really means a period, that is an elastic space of time which may be expanded or contracted to suit all requirements. But there are two fatal objections to this assumption. In the first place, the same word is rendered day in the fourth commandment, and if it means period in Genesis it means period in Exodus. In that case we are commanded to work six periods and rest on the seventh, and each period must cover a geological epoch. How pleasant for those who happen to be born in the seventh period, how unpleasant for those born in one of the six! The lives of the one class all work, those of the other all play! In the second place, the account of each day's creation concludes with the refrain "and the evening and the morning were the first (or other) day." Now evening and morning are terms which mark the luminous gradations between night and day, and these phenomena, like night and day, depend on the earth's revolving on its axis and presenting different portions of its surface to the sun. Evening and morning clearly imply a space of twenty-four hours, and the writer of Genesis, whoever he was, would probably be surprised at any other interpretation of his words. It is sometimes argued, as for instance by Dr. M'Caul, that these primeval days were of vast and unknown duration, the evening and the morning not being dependent on their present causes. But this supposition could only apply to the first three days, for the sun, moon, and stars were created on the fourth day, expressly "to rule over the day and over the night, and to divide the light from the darkness." The fifth and sixth days, at least, must be understood as of normal length, and thus the chronological difficulties remain. All animal life was brought into existence on the last two days, and therefore the Bible still allows an antiquity of less than six thousand years for the world's fauna. Geology and Biology allow millions of years. Here then Science and the Bible are in flagrant and irreconcilable contradiction.

The fact that the writer of Genesis represents light as existing three days before the creation of the sun, the source of light, has frequently been noticed. One learned commentator supposed that God had infused a certain "luminosity" through the air, which was not exactly the same as the light of the sun. But light is not a thing; it is a phenomenon caused by definite laws of astronomy and optics. Such explanations are but fanciful refuges of superstition. "God said let there be light and there was light," is not the language of science and history, but the language of poetry. As such it is sublime. We find a similar expression in the Vedas of the Hindoos: "He thought, I will create worlds, and they were there!" Both become ridiculous when presented to us as a scientific statement The physical astronomer knows how worlds are formed, as well as how their movements are determined; he knows also the causes of light; and he knows that none of these processes resembles the accounts given in the Creation Stories of the Hebrews and the Hindoos.

Science knows nothing of six creative epochs, any more than of six creative days; and it is quite certain that the order of Creation given in Genesis differs widely from the revelations of Geology. For instance (and one instance in such a case is as good as a thousand), fish and fowl are said to have been created on the same day. Let us, for the sake of argument, assume that day means period. The conclusion still is that fish and fowl were created together. Starting from this conclusion, what should we expect to find in our geological researches? Why, the fossil remains of fish and of fowl in the same epochs. But we find nothing of the kind. Marine animals antedate the carboniferous period, during which all our coal deposits were laid, but no remains of fowl are found until a later period. Now the carboniferious period alone, according to Sir William Thompson, covers many millions of years; so that instead of fish and fowl being contemporaneous, we find them geologically separated by inconceivable spaces of time. Here again the Bible and Science fatally disagree.

Even if we admit that the fifth day of creation was a period, the chronology of the Bible is still fatally at variance with fact With respect to the antiquity of the human race, it is precise and unmistakable. It gives us the age of Adam at his death, and the ages of the other antediluvian patriarchs. From the Flood the genealogies are carefully recorded, until we enter the historic period, after which there is not much room for dispute. From the creation of Adam to the birth of Christ, the Bible allows about four thousand years. The antiquity of the human race, therefore, according to Scripture, is less than six thousand years. Science, however, proves that this is but a fragment of the vast period during which man has inhabited the earth. There was a civilisation in Egypt thousands of years before the alleged creation of Adam. The Cushite civilisation was even more ancient Archaeology shows us traces of man's presence, in a ruder state, long before that. The researches of Mr. Pengelly in Kent's Cavern prove that cave-men lived there more than two-hundred thousand years ago; while geological investigations in the Valley of the Somme have established the fact that primitive men existed there in the tertiary period. Professor Draper writes:—"So far as investigations have gone, they indisputably-refer the existence of man to a date remote from us by many hundreds of thousands of years. It must be borne in mind that these investigations are quite recent, and confined to a very limited geographical space. No researches have yet been made in those regions which might reasonably be regarded as the primitive habitat of man. We are thus carried back immeasurably beyond the six thousand years of Patristic chronology. It is difficult to assign a shorter date for the last glaciation of Europe than a quarter of a million of years, and human existence antedates that. The chronology of the Bible is thus altogether obsolete."

The idea of a seven-days' creation was not confined to the Jews: it was shared by the Persians and Etruscans. The division of the year into months and weeks is a general, although not a universal practice. The ancient Egyptians observed a ten-days' week, but the seven-days' week was well known to them. The naming of the days of the week after the seven Planets was noted by Dion Cassius as originally an Egyptian custom, which spread from Egypt into the Roman Empire. The Brahmins of India also distinguish the days of the week by the planetary names. This division of time was purely astronomical. The Jews kept the Feast of the New Moon, and other of their ceremonies were determined by lunar and solar phenomena. We may be sure that the myth of a seven-days' creation followed and did not precede the regular observance of that period.

There is one feature of the Hebrew story of creation which shows how anthropomorphic they were. The Persians represent Ormuzd as keeping high festival with his angels on the seventh day, after creating all things in six. But the Hebrews represent Jehovah as resting on the seventh day, as though the arduous labors of creation had completely exhausted his energies. Fancy Omnipotence requiring rest to recruit its strength! The Bible, and especially in its earlier parts, is grossly anthropomorphic. It exhibits God as conversing with men, sharing their repasts, and helping them to slaughter their foes. It represents him as visible to human eyes, and in one instance as giving Moses a back view of his person. Yet these childish fancies are still thrust upon as divine truths, which if we disbelieve we shall be eternally damned!

Let us now examine the Creation Story internally. In the first place we find two distinct records, the one occupying the whole of the first chapter of Genesis and the first three verses of the second, at which point the other commences. These two records belong to different periods of Jewish history. The older one is the Elohistic, so called because the creator is designated by the plural term Elohim, which in our version is translated God. The more modern one is the Jehovistic, in which Elohim is combined with the singular term Jehovah, translated in our-version the Lord God. The Elohistic and Jehovistic accounts both relate the creation of man, but instead of agreeing they widely differ. The former makes God create man in his own image; the latter does not even allude to this important circumstance. The former represents man as created male and female at the outset; the latter represents the male as created first, and the female for a special reason afterwards. In the former God enjoins the primal pair to "be fruitful and multiply and replenish the earth;" in the latter there is no such injunction, but on the contrary, the bringing forth of children in sorrow is imposed upon the woman as a punishment for her sin, and she does not appear to have borne any offspring until after the expulsion from the Garden of Eden. Lastly, the Elohistic record makes no mention of this Paradise, in which, according to the Jehovistic record, the drama of the Fall was enacted, but represents man as immediately commissioned to subdue and populate the world. Such discrepancies are enough to stagger the blindest credulity.

We now proceed to examine the Jehovistic account of Creation in detail. We read that the Lord God formed man of the dust of the ground, the Hebrew word for which is adamah. The word Adam means "be red," and adamah may be referred to the red soil of Palestine. Kalisch also observes that man may have been originally called Adam on account of the red color of his skin. The Chinese represent man as kneaded of yellow earth, and the red Indians of red clay. The belief that man was formed of earth was not confined to the Jews, but has been almost universal, and undoubtedly arose from the fact that our bodies after death return to the earth and resolve into the elements. The Lord God placed this forlorn first man in the Garden of Eden with the command to till it, and permission to eat of the fruit of all its trees except "the tree of knowledge of good and evil." How Adam trespassed and fell, and brought a curse upon himself and all his innocent posterity, we shall consider in another pamphlet. The story of the Fall is infinitely curious and diverting, and must be treated separately.

Adam's first exploit, after he had taken a good look round him, was very marvellous. All the cattle and beasts of the field and fowl of the air were brought before him to be named, and "whatsover Adam called every living creature, that was the name thereof." This first Zoological Dictionary is unfortunately lost, or we should be able to call every animal by its right name, which would doubtless gratify them as well as ourselves. The fishes and insects were not included in this primitive nomenclature, so the loss of the Dictionary does not concern them.

The Lord made the animals pass before Adam seemingly with the expectation that he would choose a partner from amongst them. Nothing, however, struck his fancy. If he had fallen in love with a female gorilla or ourang-outang, what a difference it would have made in the world's history!

After this wonderful exploit "the Lord caused a deep sleep to fall upon Adam," who surely must have been tired enough to fall into a good sound natural sleep, without a heavenly narcotic. While in this state one of his ribs was extracted for a purpose we shall presently refer to, and which he discovered when he awoke. This curious surgical operation involves a dilemma. If Adam was upright after it, he must have been lopsided before; if he was upright before it, he must have been lopsided after. In either case the poor man was very scurvily treated.

It has been maintained that God provided Adam with another rib in place of the one extracted. But this is a mere conjecture. Besides, if the Lord had a spare rib in stock he might have made a woman of it, without cutting poor Adam open and making a pre mortem examination of his inside.

The divine operator's purpose was a good one, whatever we may think of his means. He had discovered, what Omniscience would have foreknown, that it was not good for man to be alone, and had resolved to make him a help-meet. Adam's "spare rib" was the raw material of which his wife was manufactured. The Greenlanders believed that the first woman was fashioned out of the man's thumb. The woman was brought to Adam, who said—"This is now bone of my bone and flesh of my flesh." Not a word did he say about "soul of my soul." Perhaps he suspected she had none, and with some truth, if we go no further than our English version. When the Lord God made man, he "breathed into his nostrils the breath of life, and man became a living soul," but apparently no such operation was performed on Eve. Indeed, it is very difficult to prove from the Bible that woman has a soul at all. Women should reflect on this. They should also reflect on the invidious fact that they were not included in the original scheme of things, but thrown in as a make-weight afterwards. Let them ponder this a while, and the churches and chapels in which this story is taught would soon be emptied. The majority of those who occupy seats in such places wear bonnets, and most of those who don't, go there for the sake of those who do.

When Adam had thus accosted his bride he grew prophetical. "Therefore," said he, "shall a man leave his father and his mother, and shall cleave unto his wife: and they shall be one flesh." In his desire to give the institution of marriage the highest sanction, the writer of this story perpetrated a gross anachronism. Adam had no parents, nor any experience of marriage. Unless, therefore, we credit him with superhuman prescience, it is absurd to make him talk in this way.

Eve's name, no less than Adam's, betrays the mythological character of the story. It means the "mother of all," and was evidently applied to her by the Jewish writers in order to signify her supposed relationship to the human race.

While God was engaged in the work of creation, why did he not make two human couples, instead of one? The arrangement he adopted involved the propagation of the human species through incest Adam and Eve's sons must have had children by their sisters. If two couples had been created, their families might have intermarried, and mankind would not then have sprang from the incestuous intercourse of the very first generation. Surely omnipotence might have obviated the necessity of a crime against which civilised consciences revolt with unspeakable disgust.

Adam and Eve were placed by God in the Garden of Eden. "Eden," says Kalisch, "comprised that tract of land where the Euphrates and Tigris separate; from that spot the 'garden in Eden' cannot be distant. Let it suffice that we know its general position." Its exact position can never be ascertained. What a pity it is that Noah did not occupy some of his leisure time, during the centuries he lived after his exit from the ark, in writing a typography of the antediluvian world! The Greeks placed Paradise in the Islands of the Blessed, beyond the Pillars of Hercules in the western main. The Swede, Rudbeck, asserts that Paradise was in Scandinavia; some Russian writers supposed it to have been in Siberia; and the German writers, Hasse and Schulz, on the coast of Prussia. Eastern traditions place it in Ceylon, and regard the mountain of Rahoun as the spot where Adam was buried. Some old Christian writers hazarded the theory that Paradise was beyond the earth altogether, on the other side of the ocean which they conceived to encircle it, and that Noah was conveyed to our planet by the deluge. Kalisch gives a long list of ancient and modern authorities on the subject, who differ widely from each other as to the actual position of Eden, their only point of agreement being that it was somewhere.

The Creation Story of the Bible cannot be considered as anything but a Hebrew myth. Scholars have abundantly shown the absurdity of supposing that Moses wrote it. Doubtless, as a piece of traditional mythology, it is very ancient, but it cannot be traced back in its present literary form beyond the Babylonish captivity. Men of science without exception disbelieve it, not only with regard to the world in general, but also with regard to the human race. In his famous article on "The Method and Results of Ethnology," Professor Huxley made this declaration:—"There are those who represent the most numerous, respectable, and would-be orthodox of the public, and who may be called 'Adamites,' pure and simple. They believe that Adam was made out of earth somewhere in Asia, about six thousand years ago; that Eve was modelled from one of his ribs; and that the progeny of these two having been reduced to the eight persons who landed on the summit of Mount Ararat after an universal deluge, all the nations of the earth have proceeded from these last, have migrated to their present localities, and have become converted into negroes, Australians, Mongolians, etc., within that time. Five-sixths of the public are taught this Adamitic Monogenism as if it were an established truth, and believe it. I do not; and I am not acquainted with any man of science, or duly instructed person, who does." The clergy, then, who go on teaching this old Creation Story as true, are either unduly instructed or dishonest, ignorant or fraudulent, blind guides or base deceivers. It is not for us to determine to which class any priest or preacher belongs: let the conscience of each, as assuredly it will, decide that for himself. But ignorant or dishonest, we affirm, is every one of them who still teaches the Creation Story as a record of actual facts, or as anything but a Hebrew myth.

The origin of the human race is far different from that recorded in Genesis. Man has undoubtedly been developed from a lower form of life. The rude remains of primitive men show that they were vastly inferior to the present civilised inhabitants of the world, and even inferior to the lowest savages with whom we are now acquainted. Their physical and mental condition was not far removed from that of the higher apes; and the general opinion of biologists is that they were descended from the Old World branch of the great Simian family. There is, indeed, no absolute proof of this, nor is it probable that there ever will be, as the fossil links between primitive man and his Simian progenitor, if they exist at all, are most likely buried in that sunken continent over which roll the waters of the South Pacific Ocean. But as the line of natural development can be carried back so far without break, there is no reason why it should not be carried farther. The evolution theory is now almost universally accepted by men of science, and few of them suppose that man can be exempted from the general laws of biology. At any rate, the Bible account of Creation is thoroughly exploded, and when that is gone there is nothing to hinder our complete acceptance of the only theory of man's origin which is consistent with the facts of his history, and explains the peculiarities of his physical structure.

NOAH'S FLOOD

The Bible story of the Deluge is at once the biggest and the most ridiculous in the whole volume. Any person who reads it with the eyes of common sense, and some slight knowledge of science, must admit that it is altogether incredible and absurd, and that the book which contains it cannot be the Word of God.

About 1,656 years after God created Adam, and placed him in the garden of Eden, the world had become populous and extremely wicked; indeed, every thought and imagination of man's heart was evil continually. What was the cause of all this wickedness we are not informed; but we are told that the sons of God took unto them wives of the daughters of men because they were fair, and we are led to suppose that these matches produced giants and other incurably wicked offspring. No physiological reason is assigned for this Strange result, nor perhaps was there any present to the mind of the writer, who probably had witnessed unhappy marriages in his own family, and was anxious to warn his readers, however vaguely, against allowing their daughters to be inveigled into matrimonial bonds with pious sniffling fellows, who professed themselves peculiarly the children of their Father in heaven. However, the narrative is clear as to the fact itself: men had all gone irrecoverably astray, and God had repented that he ever made them. In such a case an earthly human father would naturally have attempted to improve his family; but the Almighty Father either was too indifferent to do so, or was too well aware of the impossibility of reforming his own wretched offspring; and therefore he determined to drown them all at one fell swoop, just as cat-loving old ladies dispose of a too numerous and embarrassing feline progeny. Bethinking him, however, God resolved to save alive one family to perpetuate the race: he was willing to give his creatures another chance, and then, if they persisted in going the wrong way, it would still be easy to drown the lot of them again, and that without any reservation. He had also resolved at first to destroy every living thing from off the face of the earth; but he afterwards decided to spare from destruction two of every species of unclean beasts, male and female, and fourteen, male and female, of all clean beasts and of all fowls of the air and of every creeping thing. Noah, his wife, his three sons, Shem, Ham, and Japhet, and their wives (eight persons in all), were the only human beings to be preserved from the terrible fate of drowning.

Noah was commanded by God to build an ark for the reception of the precious living freight, the dimensions of which were to be, in English measure, 550 feet long, 93 feet wide, and 55 feet deep. Into this floating box they all got; the flood then came and covered the earth, and all besides were drowned.

Now this is a very strange, a very startling story; it seems more like a chapter from the "Arabian Nights" or the "Adventures of Baron Munchausen" than from the sacred Scriptures of any Religion. Carnal reason prompts us to ask many questions about it.

1. How did Noah contrive to bring these beasts, birds, and insects all together in one spot? The task seems superhuman. Some species could be found only in very remote places—the kangaroo only in Australia, the sloth only in South America, the polar bear only in the Arctic regions. How could Noah, in those days of difficult locomotion, have journeyed in search of these across broad rivers, and over continents and oceans? Did he bring them singly to his dwelling-place in Asia, or did he travel hither and thither with his menagerie, and finish the collection before returning home? There are, according to Hugh Miller, 1,658 known species of mammalia, 6,266 of birds, 642 of reptiles, and 550,000 of insects; how could one man, or a hundred men, have collected specimens of these in those days, and in such & brief space of time? The beasts, clean and unclean, male and female, might be got together by means of terrible exertion; but surely to assemble the birds and reptiles and insects must transcend human capacity. Some of the last class

would of course not require much seeking; they visit us whether we desire their company or not; and the difficulty would not be how to get them into the ark, but how on earth to keep them out. Others, however, would give infinite trouble. Fancy Noah occupied in a wild-goose chase, or selecting specimens from a wasps' or hornets' nest, or giving assiduous chase to a vigilant and elusive bluebottle fly!

But suppose Noah to have succeeded in his arduous enterprise, the question still remains, how did he keep his wonderful zoological collection alive? Some of them could live only in certain latitudes; the inhabitants of cold climates would melt away amidst the torrid heat of Central Asia. Then, again, there are some insects that live only a few hours, and some that live a few days at the utmost: what means were adopted for preserving these? Some animals, too, do not pair, but run in herds; many species of fish swim in shoals; sometimes males and sometimes females predominate, as in the case of deer, where one male heads and appropriates a whole herd of females, or in the case of bees, where many males are devoted to the queen of the hive. These could not have gone in pairs, or lived in pairs; their instincts pointed to another method of grouping. How did Noah provide for their due preservation? When these questions are answered others speedily arise; in fact, there is no end to the difficulties of this marvellous story.

2. Whence and how did Noah procure the food for his huge menagerie? That he was obliged to do so, that the animals were not miraculously preserved without food, we are certain; for he was expressly commanded by God to gather food for himself and for them. "Take thou unto thee," it was said to him, "of all food that is eaten, and thou shalt gather it to thee; and it shall be for food for thee, and for them." What provision was made for the carnivorous animals, for lions, tigers, vultures, kites, and hawks? Some of these would require not simply meat, but fresh meat, which could not be provided for them unless superfluous animals were taken into the ark to be killed, or Noah had learned the art of potting flesh. Otters would require fish, chameleons flies, woodpeckers grubs, night-

hawks moths, and humming-birds the honey of flowers. What vast quantities of water also would be consumed! In fact, the task of collecting food to last all the inmates of the ark, including the eight human beings, for more than a year, must have been greater even than that of bringing them together in the first place from every zone. The labors of Hercules were mere trifles compared with those of Noah. Poor old patriarch! He amply earned his salvation. Had he been possessed of one tithe of Jacob's cunning and business sagacity, he would have struck a better bargain with God, and have got into the ark on somewhat easier terms. Few men would have undertaken so much to gain so little.

3. How were all the animals, with their food, got into the ark? The dimensions as given in the Bible would be insufficient to accommodate a tithe of them; the ark could not have contained them all, if they were packed together like herrings or sardines. Even if they were so packed, space would still be required for their food; and for what a vast quantity! An animal even with man's moderate appetite would consume in the course of twelve months solid matter to the extent of four or five times its own weight, and some animals are of course far more voracious. This difficulty as to stowing the animals and their food into the ark is quite insuperable; it is not to be obviated by any employment of miraculous intervention. Not even omnipotence can make a clock strike less than one, and God himself must fail to make two things occupy the same space at the same time.

4. How where the inmates of this floating menagerie, supposing them got in, supplied with fresh air? According to the Bible narrative the ark was furnished with but one window of a cubit square, and one door which was shut by God himself, and it may be presumed, quite securely fastened. Talk about the Black-hole of Calcutta, why it was nothing to this! What a scramble there must have been for that solitary window and a mouthful of fresh air! Lions, tigers, jackals, hyaenas, boa-constrictors, kangaroos, eagles, owls, bees, wasps, bluebottles, with Noah, Shem, Ham, and Japhet, and their wives, all in one fierce melee. But the contention for the

precious vital air must, however violent, have soon subsided: fifteen minutes would have settled them all. Yet curiously enough the choking animals-suffered no appreciable injury; by some occult means they were all preserved from harm; which furnishes another illustration of the mysterious ways of God. What powerful perfumes, too, must have arisen from all those animals! So powerful indeed that even the rancid flavor of foxes and skunks must have been undistinguishable from the blended scents of all their fellow passengers. Those who have visited Wombwell's menagerie, or stood in the monkey-house of the Zoological Gardens, doubtless retain a lively recollection of olfactory disgust, even although in those places the must scrupulous cleanliness is observed; but their experience of such smells would have been totally eclipsed if they could but for a moment have stood within Noah's ark amidst all its heterogeneous denizens. However the patriarch and his sons managed to cleanse this worse than Augean stable passes all understanding. And then what trampings they must have had up and down those flights of stairs communicating with the three storeys of the ark, in order to cast all the filth out of that one window. No wonder their children afterwards began to build a tower of Babel to reach unto heaven; it was quite natural that they should desire plenty of steps, to mount, so as to gratify fully the itch of climbing they had inherited from their parents.

5. Where did all the water come from? According to the Bible story the waters prevailed upon the earth a hundred and fifty days, and covered all the high hills and mountains under the whole heaven. Now mount Ararat itself, on which the Ark eventually rested, is seventeen thousand feet high, and the utmost peaks of Himalaya are nearly twice as high as that; and to cover the whole earth with water to such a tremendous height would require an immense quantity of water; in fact, about eight times as much as is contained in all the rivers, lakes, seas, and oceans of our globe. Whence did all this water come? The Scripture explanation is sadly insufficient; the fountains of the great deep were broken up, and the windows of heaven were opened, and the rain was upon the earth for forty days and forty nights. The writer evidently thought that there were great

fountains at the bottom of the sea, capable of supplying water in unlimited quantities from some central reservoir; but science knows nothing whatever about them; nay, science tells us that the internal reservoir, if there be one, must contain not water, but liquid fire. If this great reservoir poured its contents into the sea, the result would be similar to that frightful catastrophe imagined by the Yankee who wished to see Niagara Falls pour into Mount Vesuvius.

The supply from that quarter thus failing, we are forced back upon the rain which descended from the windows of heaven, wherever they may be. It rained forty days and forty nights. Forty days and forty nights! Why forty million days and nights of rain would not have sufficed. The writer was evidently in total ignorance of the laws of hydrology. The rain which falls from the clouds originally comes from the waters of the earth, being absorbed into the atmosphere by the process of evaporation. The utmost quantity of water that can thus be held in suspense throughout the entire atmosphere is very small; in fact, if precipitated, it would only cover the ground to the depth of about five inches. After the first precipitation of rain, the process of evaporation would have to be repeated; that is, for every additional descent of rain a proportionate quantity of water would have to be extracted from the rivers, lakes, and seas below. Now, surely every sane man must perceive that this pretty juggle could not add one single drop to the previously existing amount of water, any more than a man could make himself rich by taking money out of one pocket and putting it into another. The fabled man who is reported to have occupied himself with dipping up water from one side of a boat and emptying it over on the other, hoping thereby to bale the ocean dry, must have been the real author of this story of Noah and his wonderful ark.

Some Christian writers, such as Dr. Pye Smith, Dr. Barry, and Hugh Miller, have contended that the author of the book of Genesis is describing not a universal but a partial deluge; not a flood which submerged the whole earth, out one that merely covered some particular part of the great Central Asian plains. But surely, apart from any consideration pertaining to the very emphatic language of the text, rational men must perceive that the difficulty is not obviated by this explanation, but rather increased. How could the waters ascend in one place to the height of seventeen thousand feet (the height of Mount Ararat) without overflowing the adjacent districts, and, indeed, the whole earth, in conformity to the law of gravitation? Delitzch is bold enough to assert that the flood of water was ejected with such force from the fountains beneath that it assumed quite naturally a conical shape. But then, even supposing that this explication were anything but sheer silliness, which it is not, how would the learned commentator account for the water retaining its conical shape for months after the force of upheaval had expended itself? These explanations are entirely fanciful and groundless. The language of the narrative is sufficiently explicit "And all flesh died that moved upon the earth;" "all in whose nostrils was the breath of life;" "and every living substance was destroyed which was upon the face of the ground;" and "Noah only remained alive and they that were with him in the ark." Such are the precise unmistakeable words of Scripture, which no sophistry can explain away. But even if the contention for a partial deluge could be made good, the fundamental difficulties would still remain. As Colenso observes, the flood, "whether it be regarded as a universal or a partial deluge, is equally incredible and impossible."

Geology absolutely contradicts the possibility of any such catastrophe as the deluge within the historic period. According to Sir Charles Lyell, no devastating flood could have passed over the forest zone of Ætna during the last twelve thousand years; and the volcanic cones of Auvergne, which enclose in their ashes the remains of extinct animals, and present an outline as perfect as that of Ætna, are deemed older still. Kalisch forcibly presents this aspect of the question: "Geology teaches the impossibility of a universal deluge since the last six thousand years, but does not exclude a partial destruction of the earth's surface within that period. The Biblical text, on the other hand, demands the supposition of a universal deluge, and absolutely excludes a partial flood."

6. What became of all the fish? In such a deluge the rivers and seas must have mingled their waters, and this, in conjunction with the terrific outpour from the windows of heaven, must have made the water brackish, too salt for fresh-water fish, and too fresh for salt-water fish; and consequently the aquatic animals must all have perished, unless, indeed, they were miraculously preserved—a contingency which anyone is free to conjecture, out no one is at liberty to assert, seeing that the inspired writer never even hints such a possibility. Now there is no evidence whatever that Noah took and fish with him into the ark; under natural circumstances they must have perished outside; yet the seas and rivers still teem with life. When did the new creation of fish take place?

7. What became of all the vegetation? Every particle of it must have rotted during such a long submergence. But even if mysteriously preserved from natural decay, it must still have been compressed into a mere pulp by the terrific weight of the super-incumbent water. Colenso estimates that the pressure of a column of water 17,000 feet high would be 474 tons upon each square foot of surface—a pressure which nothing could have resisted. Yet, wonderful to relate, just prior to the resting of the ark on Mount Ararat, the dove sent out therefrom returned with an olive leaf in her mouth just pluckt off. A fitting climax to this wonderful story.

Finally the story relates how the ark rested on the top of Mount Ararat, whence its inmates descended to the plains below, which were then quite dry. Mount Ararat towers aloft three thousand feet above the region of eternal snow. How the poor animals, aye, even the polar bear, must have shivered! And what a curious sight it must have been to witness their descent from such a height Often have I speculated on the probable way in which the elephant got down, and after much careful thought I have concluded thus: either he had waxed so fat with being fed so long on miraculous food that he rolled pleasantly down like a ball, with no other injury than a few scratches; or he had become so very, very thin with living simply on expectations, in default of more substantial fare, that he gently floated down by virtue of levity, like a descending feather.

And then what journeys some of the poor animals would have to make; the kangaroo back to Australia, the sloth to South America, the polar bear to the extreme north. How they lived on the road to their ultimate destinations the Lord only knows. There was no food for them; the deluge had destroyed all vegetation for the herbiverous animals, all flesh for the carniverous. Not even a nibble was left for the sheep.

As for poor Noah, the first thing recorded of him after his watery expedition is that he drank heavily of wine and got into a state of beastly inebriation. And who can wonder that he did so? The poor old man had floated about on oceans of water for more than a year, and probably he was heartily sick of his watery prospect. The astonishing thing is that he did not get water on the brain. It was quite natural that he should swill deep potations of some stronger fluid on the first available opportunity. Surely he had water enough during that twelve months to last a lifetime; enough to justify his never touching the wretched fluid again.

While Noah was dead drunk, his second son. Ham, saw "the nakedness of his father," and reported the fact to his two brethren, who took a garment and, walking backwards so that they might not see, covered the patriarch's nudity. On recovering from his drunken stupor, Noah discovered "what his younger son had done unto him," and proceeded at once to vigorous cursing. Ham was the offender, if there was any offence at all, which is not very clear; but punishment in the Bible is generally vicarious, and we read that the irate patriarch cursed Canaan, the son of Ham, for his father's misdemeanor. Flagitiously unjust as it is, this proceeding thoroughly accords with Jehovah's treatment of Adam's posterity after he and Eve had committed their first sin by eating of the forbidden fruit.

Before Noah got drunk he had received from God the assurance that the world should never more be destroyed by a flood. As a perpetual sign of this covenant the rainbow was set in the heavens. But the rainbow must have been a common sight for centuries before. This phenomenon of refraction is the result of natural causes which operated before the Flood, as well as after. The earth yielded its fruits for human sustenance, and therefore rain must have fallen. If rain fell before the Deluge, as we are bound to conclude, the rainbow must have been then as now. The usual practice of commentators is to explain this portion of the narrative by assuming that the rainbow was visible before the covenant with Noah, but only after the covenant had a special significance. But, as Colenso observes, the writer of the story supposes the rainbow was then first set in the clouds, and is evidently accounting for the origin of this beautiful phenomenon, which might well appear supernatural to his uninstructed imagination.

Besides the manifold absurdities of this story there are other aspects of it even more startling. What a picture it presents of fiendish cruelty and atrocious vindictiveness! What an appalling exhibition of divine malignity! God, the omnipotent and omniscient ruler of the universe, is represented as harboring and executing the most diabolical intentions. He ruthlessly exterminates all his children except a favored few, and includes in his vengeance the lower animals also, although they were innocent of offence against his laws. Every creature in whose nostrils was the breath of life, with the exception of those persevered in the ark, was drowned, and the earth was turned into a vast slaughter-house. How imagination pictures the terrible scene as the waters rise higher and higher, and the ravening waves speed after their prey! Here some wretched being, baffled and hopeless, drops supinely into the raging flood; there a stronger and stouter heart struggles to the last. Here selfish ones battling for their own preservation; there husbands and wives, parents and children, lovers and maidens, affording mutual aid, or at last, in utter despair, locked in a final embrace and meeting death together. And when the waters subside, what a sickening scene presents itself! Those plains, once decked with verdure, and lovely in the sun and breeze, are covered with the bones of a slaughtered world. How can the Christian dare to justify such awful cruelty? The God of the Pentateuch is not a beneficent universal father, but an almighty fiend.

This story of Noah's Flood is believed still because people never examine what is taught them as the word of God. Every one who analyses the story must pronounce it the most extraordinary amalgam of immorality and absurdity ever palmed off on a credulous world.

EVE AND THE APPLE

Christianity is based upon the story of the Fall. In Adam all sinned, as in Christ all must be sayed. Saint Paul gives to this doctrine the high sanction of his name, and we may disregard the puny whipsters of theology, who, without any claim to inspiration, endeavor to explain the Genesaic narrative as an allegory rather than a history. If Adam did not really fall he could not have been cursed for falling, and his posterity could not have become partakers either in a sin which was never committed or in a malediction which was never pronounced. Nor can Original Sin be a true dogma if our first parents did not transmit the germs of iniquity to their children. If Adam did not fall there was no need for Christ to save us; if he did not set God and man at variance there was no need for an atonement; and so the Christian scheme of salvation would be a fiasco from beginning to end. This will never do. No Garden of Eden, no Gethsemane! No Fall, no Redemption! No Adam, no Christ!

Mother Eve's curiosity was the motive of the first transgression of God's commandments in the history of the world, and the whole human race was brought under the risk of eternal perdition because of her partiality to fruit. Millions of souls now writhe in hell because, six thousand years ago, she took a bite of an apple. What a tender and beautiful story! God made her to be Adam's helpmeet. She helped him to a slice of apple, and that soon helped them both outside Eden. The sour stuff disagreed with him as it did with her. It has disagreed, with all their posterity. In fact it was endowed with the marvellous power of transmitting spiritual stomach-ache through any number of generations.

How do we know that it was an apple and not some other fruit? Why, on the best authority extant after the Holy Scriptures themselves, namely, our auxiliary Bible, "Paradise Lost;" in the tenth book whereof Satan makes the following boast to his infernal peers after his exploit in Eden:—

> *"Him by fraud I have seduced*
> *From his Creator, and, the more to increase*
> *Your wonder, with an apple."*

Yet another authority is the profane author of "Don Juan," who, in the first stanza of the tenth canto, says of Newton:

> *"And this is the sole mortal who could grapple,*
> *Since Adam, with a fall, or with an apple."*

Milton, being very pious, was probably in the counsel of God. How else could he have given us an authentic version of the long colloquies that were carried on in heaven? Byron, being very profane, was probably in the counsel of Satan. And thus we have the most unimpeachable testimony of two opposite sources to the fact that it was an apple, and not a rarer fruit, which overcame the virtue of our first parents, and played the devil with their big family of children.

This apple grew on the Tree of Knowledge, which God planted in the midst of the Garden of Eden, sternly enjoining Adam and Eve not to eat of its fruit under pain of death. Now the poor woman knew nothing of death and could not understand what a dreadful punishment it was; and there was the fruit dangling before her eyes every hour of the day. Is it any wonder that she brooded incessantly on the one thing forbidden, that her woman's curiosity was irresistably piqued by it, and that at last her longing grew so intense that she exclaimed, "Dear me! I can't refrain any longer. Let the consequences be what they will, I must have a bite." God made the woman; he knew her weakness; and he must have known that the plan he devised to test her obedience was the most certain trap that could be invented. Jehovah played with poor Eve just as a cat plays with a mouse. She had free-will, say the theologians. Yes, and so has the mouse a free run. But the cat knows she can catch it again, and finish it off when she is tired of playing.

Not only did God allow Eve's curiosity to urge her on to sin, he also permitted the serpent, "more subtil than any beast of the field," to supplement its action. This wily creature is popularly supposed to have been animated on the occasion by the Devil himself; although, as we shall explain in another Romance entitled "The Bible Devil," the book of Genesis makes not even the remotest allusion to such a personage. If, however, the tempter was the Devil, what chance had the poor woman against his seductive wiles? And even if he was only a serpent, he was very "subtil" as we are told, and able to talk like a book, and we know that these creatures have fatal powers of fascination. Surely Mother Eve was heavily handicapped. God might have given her fair play, and left her to fight the battle without furnishing auxiliaries to the strong side.

The serpent, we have said, could converse in human speech. His conversation and his conduct will be dealt with in the Romance just referred to. Suffice it here to say that he plainly told the woman that God was a liar. "He," said the tempter, "has said ye shall surely die if ye touch the fruit of this tree. Don't believe it. I tell you, ye shall not surely die." What could poor Eve think? In addition to her native curiosity here was another incentive to disobedience. Which of these two spoke the truth? There was only one way of deciding. She stretched forth her hand, plucked an apple, and began to eat. And immediately, says Milton,

> *"Earth felt the wound, and nature from her seat,*
> *Sighing through all her works, gave signs of woe*
> *That all was lost."*

What a rumpus about a trifle! It reminds us of the story of a Jew who had a sneaking inclination for a certain meat prohibited by his creed. One day the temptation to partake was too strong; he slipped into a place of refreshment and ordered some sausages. The weather happened to be tempestuous, and just as he raised his knife and fork to attack the savory morsel, a violent clap of thunder nearly frightened him out of his senses. Gathering courage, he essayed a second time, but another thunderclap warned him to desist. A third attempt was foiled in the same way. Whereupon he threw down his knife and fork and made for the door, exclaiming "What a dreadful fuss about a little bit of pork."

Eve's transgression, according to the learned Lightfoot, occurred "about high noone, the time of eating." The same authority informs us that she and Adam "did lie comfortlesse, till towards the cool of the day, or three o'clock afternoon." However that may be, it is most certain that the first woman speedily got the better of the first man. She told him the apple was nice and he took a bite also. Perhaps he had resolved to share her fortunes good or bad, and objected to be left alone with his menagerie. Lightfoot describes the wife as "the weaker vessell," but a lady friend of ours says that the Devil stormed the citadel first, knowing well that such a poor outpost as Adam could easily be carried afterwards.

Having eaten of the fruit, and thus learned to distinguish between good and evil, Adam and Eve quickly discovered that they were naked. So they "sewed fig leaves together, and made themselves aprons." We are not told who gave them lessons in sewing. Perhaps they acquired the art through intuition. But the necessary implements could not have been gained in that way. Dr. Thomas Burnet, whose mind was greatly exercised by the astounding wonders of the Bible, very pertinently asked "Whence had they a needle, whence a thread, on the first day of their creation?" He, however, could give no answer to the question, nor can we, except we suppose that some of the female angels had attended a "garden party" in Eden and carelessly left their needles and thread behind them. Any reader who is dissatisfied with this explanation must inquire of the nearest parson, who, as he belongs to a class supposed to know almost everything, and believed to have access to the oracles of God, will doubtless be able to reveal the whole gospel truth on the subject.

A little later, God himself, who is everywhere at once, came down from everywhere to the Garden of Eden, for the purpose of taking a "walk in the cool of the day." He had perhaps just visited the infernal regions to see that everything was ready for the reception of the miserable creatures he meant to damn, or to assure himself that the Devil was really not at home; and was anxious to cool himself before returning to his celestial abode, as well as to purify himself from the sulphurous taint which might else have sent a shudder through all the seraphic hosts. Apparently he was holding a soliloquy, for Adam and Eve "heard his voice." Colenso, however, renders this portion of the Romance differently from our authorised version—"And they heard the sound of Jehovah-Elohim walking in the garden in the breeze of the day." Delitzsch thinks they heard the sound of his footsteps, for God used to visit them in the form of a man! Could the force of folly farther go? Any devout Theist, who candidly thought over this petty fiction, would find its gross anthropomorphism inexpressibly shocking.

Knowing that God was everywhere, Adam and Eve nevertheless "hid themselves from the presence of the Lord God amongst the trees of the garden." But they were soon dragged forth to the light. Adam, who seems to have been a silly fellow, explained that he had hidden himself because he was naked, as though the Lord had not seen him in that state before. "Naked!" said the Lord, "Who told thee that thou wast naked. Hast thou eaten of that tree, eh?" "O, Lord, yes," replied Adam; "just a little bit; but it wasn't my fault, she made me do it, O Lord! O Lord!" Whereupon God, who although he knows everything, even before it happens, was singularly ill-informed on this occasion, turned fiercely upon the woman, asking her what she had done. "Oh, if you please," whimpered poor Eve, "it was I who took the first bite; but the serpent beguiled me, and the fault you see is not mine but his. Oh dear! oh dear!" Then the Lord utterly lost his temper. He cursed the serpent, cursed the woman, cursed the man, and even cursed the ground beneath their feet Everything about at the time came in for a share of the malison. In fact, it was what the Yankees would call a good, all-round, level swear.

The curse of the serpent is a subject we must reserve for our pamphlet on "The Bible Devil," The curse of the woman was that she should bring forth children in pain and sorrow, and that the man should rule over her. With her present physiological condition, woman must always have suffered during conception as she now does; and therefore Delitzsch infers that her structure must have undergone a change, although he cannot say in what respect He dwells also on the "subjection" of woman, which "the religion of Revelation" has made by degrees more endurable; probably forgetting that the Teutonic women of ancient times were regarded with veneration, long before Christianity originated. Besides, the subordination of the female is not peculiar to the human race, but is the general law throughout the animal world.

Adam's curse was less severe. He was doomed to till the ground, and to earn his bread by the sweat of his face. Most of us would rather take part in the great strenuous battle of life, than loll about under the trees in the Garden of Eden, chewing the cud like contemplative cows. What men have had to complain of in all ages is, not that they have to earn their living by labour, but that when the sweat of their faces has been plenteously poured forth the "bread" has too often not accrued to them as the reward of their industry.

Orthodox Christianity avers that all the posterity of Adam and Eve necessarily participate in their curse, and the doctrine of Original Sin is taught from all its pulpits. Only by baptism can the stains of our native guilt be effaced; and thus the unbaptized, even infants, perish everlastingly, and hell, to use the words of a Protestant divine, holds many a babe not a span long. A great Catholic divine says—"Hold thou most firmly, nor do thou in any respect doubt, that infants, whether in their mothers' wombs they begin to live and then die, or when, after their mothers have given birth to them, they pass from this life without the sacrament of holy baptism, will be punished with the everlasting punishment of eternal fire." Horror of horrors! These men call sceptics blasphemers, but they are the real blasphemers when they attribute to their God such supreme injustice and cruelty. What should we think of a legislator who proposed that the descendants of all thieves should be imprisoned, and the descendants of all murderers hung? We should think that he was bad or mad. Yet this is precisely analogous to the conduct ascribed to God, who should be infinitely wiser than the wisest man and infinitely better than the best.

The crime of our first parents was indeed pregnant with the direst consequences. It not only induced the seeds of original sin, but it also brought death into the world. Milton sings—

> "Of man's first disobedience,
> And the fruit Of that forbidden tree,
> Whose mortal taste
> Brought death into the world."

And Saint Paul (Romans v., 12) writes "As by one man sin came into the world, and death by sin."

Now this theory implies that before the Fall the inhabited portion of the world was the scene of perfect peace. Birds lived on seeds and eschewed worms, and the fierce carniverous animals grazed like oxen. The lion laid down with the lamb. "Waal," said the Yankee, "I don't doubt that, but I rayther guess the lamb was inside." The fact is that most of the carnivorous animals could not live on a vegetable drat; and therefore they must either have subsisted on flesh before the Fall, which of course involves death, or their natures must have undergone a radical change. The first supposition contradicts scripture, and the second contradicts science.

Geology shows us that in the very earliest times living creatures died from the same causes which kill them now. Many were overwhelmed by floods and volcanoes, or engulphed by earthquakes; many died of old age or disease, for their bones are found distorted or carious, and their limbs twisted with pain; while the greater number were devoured, according to the general law of the struggle for existence. Death ruled universally before the human race made its appearance on the earth, and has absolutely nothing to do with Eve and her apple.

Adam and Eve were warned by God that in the day they ate of the fruit of the Tree of Knowledge they should surely die. The serpent declared this to be rank nonsense, and the event proved his veracity. What age Eve attained to the Holy Bible saith not, for it never considers women of sufficient importance to have their longevities chronicled. But Adam lived to the remarkably good old age of nine hundred and thirty years. Like our Charles the Second he took "an unconscionable time a-dying." One of his descendants, the famous Methusaleh, lived thirty-nine years longer; while the more famous Melchizedek is not even dead yet, if any credence is to be placed in the words of holy Saint Paul.

But all these are mere lambs, infants, or chicken, in comparison with the primeval patriarchs of India. Buckle tells us that, according to the Hindoos, common men in ancient times lived to the age of 80,000 years, some dying a little sooner and some a little later. Two of their kings, Yudhishther and Alarka, reigned respectively 27,000 and 66,000 years. Both these were cut off in their prime; for some of the early poets lived to be about half a million; while one king, the most virtuous as well as the most remarkable of all, was two million years old when he began to reign, and after reigning 6,800,000 years, he resigned his empire and lingered on for 100,000 years more. Adam is not in the hunt with that tough old fellow. On the principle that it is as well to be hung for a sheep as a lamb, faithful Christians should swallow him as well as Adam. When the throat of their credulity is once distended they may as well take in everything that comes. What followed the Curse clearly shows that man was not originally created immortal. Adam and Eve were expelled from the Garden of Eden expressly in order that they might not become so. God "drove them forth" lest they should "take also of the tree of life, and eat, and live for ever." Many orthodox writers, who have to maintain the doctrine of our natural immortality, preserve a discreet silence on this text. Our great Milton, who has so largely determined the Protestant theology of

England, goes right in the face of Scripture when he makes God say of man,

> "I at first with two fair gifts
> Created him endowed, with happiness
> And immortality."

The fact is, the Book of Genesis never once alludes to any such thing, nor does it represent man as endowed with any other soul than that "breath of life" given to all animals. It is also certain that the ancient Jews were entirely ignorant of the doctrine of a life beyond the grave. The highest promise that Moses is said to have made in the Decalogue was that their "days should be long in the land." The Jews were a business people, and they wanted all promises fulfilled on this side of death.

Nor is there any real Fall implied in this story. God himself says that "the man," having eaten of the forbidden fruit, "is become as one of us." That could scarcely be a fall which brought him nearer to God. Bishop South, indeed, in a very eloquent passage of his sermon on "Man Created in God's Image," celebrates the inconceivable perfection of the first man, and concludes by saying that "An Aristotle was but the rubbish of an Adam, and Athens but the rudiments of Paradise." But a candid perusal of Genesis obliges us to dissent from this view, Adam and Eve were a very childish pair. Whatever intellect they possessed they carefully concealed. Not a scintillation of it has reached us. Shakespeare and Newton are an infinite improvement on Adam and Eve. One of the Gnostic sects, who played such havoc with the early Christian Church, utterly rejected the idea of a Fall. "The Ophites," says Didron, "considered the God of the Jews not only to be a most wicked but an unintelligent being.... According to their account, Jalda-baoth, the wicked demi-god adored by the Jews under the name of Jehovah, was jealous of man, and wished to prevent the progress of knowledge; but the serpent, the agent of superior wisdom, came to teach man what course he ought to pursue, and by what means he might regain the knowledge of good and evil. The Ophites consequently adored the serpent, and cursed the true God Jehovah."

Before expelling Adam and Eve from Eden, the Lord took pity on their nakedness, and apparently seeing that their skill in needlework did not go beyond aprons, he "made coats of skins, and clothed them." Jehovah was thus the first tailor, and the prototype of that imperishable class of workmen, of whom it was said that it takes nine of them to make a man. He was also the first butcher and the first tanner, for he must have slain the animals and dressed their skins.

Lest they should return he "placed at the east of the Garden of Eden Cherubims, and a flaming sword which turned every way, to keep the way of the tree of life." As this guard seems never to have been relieved, profane wits have speculated whether the Flood drowned them, and quenched the flaming sword with a great hiss. Ezekiel describes the Cherubims with characteristic magnificence. These creatures with wings and wheels were "full of eyes round about." And "everyone had low faces: the first face was the face of a cherub, and the second face was the face of a man, and the third the face of a lion, and the fourth the face of an eagle." What monsters! No wonder they effectually frightened poor Adam and Eve from attempting a re-entrance into the Garden.

Perhaps the reader would like to know what became of the Tree of Knowledge. One legend of the Middle Ages relates that Eve along with the forbidden fruit broke off a branch which she carried with her from Paradise. Planted outside by her hand, it grew to a great tree, under which Abel was killed; at a later time it was used in building the most holy place of Solomon's temple; and finally it yielded the beams out of which the cross was made! Another legend says that, after the Fall, God rooted out the Tree of Knowledge, and flung it over the wall of Paradise. A thousand years after it was found by Abraham, none the worse for its long absence from the soil. He planted it in his garden, and while doing so he was informed by a voice from heaven that this was the tree on whose wood the Redeemer should be crucified.

Space does not allow us to dwell at length on the Paradise Myths of other ancient peoples, which singularly resembled that of the Jews. Formerly it was alleged that these were all corruptions of the Genesaic story. But it is now known that most of them date long anterior to the very existence of the Jewish people. As Kalisch says, "they belonged to the common traditionary lore of the Asiatic nations." The Bible story of Paradise is derived almost entirely from the Persian myth. It was after contact with the reformed religion of Zoroaster, during their captivity, that the remnant of the Jews who returned to Palestine collated their ancient literature, and revised it in accordance with their new ideas. The story of Eve and her Apple is, as every scholar knows, an oriental myth slightly altered by the Jewish scribes to suit the national taste, and has absolutely no claims on our credence. And if this be so, the doctrine of the Fall collapses, and down comes the whole Christian structure which is erected upon it.

THE BIBLE DEVIL

The Christian Godhead is usually spoken and written of as a Trinity, whereas it is in fact a Quaternion, consisting of God the Father, God the Son, God the Holy Ghost, and God the Devil. The Roman Catholics add yet another, Goddess the Virgin Mary. God the Devil, whom this Romance treats of so far as his history is contained in the Bible, is popularly supposed to be inferior to the other persons of the Godhead. In reality, however, he is vastly their superior both in wisdom and in power. For, whereas they made the world, he has appropriated it almost entirely to himself; and, whereas they who created all its inhabitants, have only been able to lay down a very narrow-gauge railway to the Kingdom of Heaven, he has contrived to lay down an exceedingly broad-gauge railway to the Kingdom of Hell. Few passengers travel by their route, and its terminus on this side is miserably small; but his route is almost universally patronised, its terminus is magnificent, and there is an extraordinary rush for tickets.

According to the Christian scheme, the Devil tempted Adam and Eve from their allegiance to God in the form of a serpent. He played the devil with Eve, she played the devil with Adam, and together they have played the Devil with the whole human race ever since.

But let any unbiassed person read the Genesaic story of the Fall, and he will certainly discover no reference to the Devil A serpent is spoken of as "more subtle than any beast of the field;" it is throughout represented simply as a serpent; and nowhere is there the faintest indication of its possessing any supernatural endowments.

The Story of the Fall contains clear relics of that Tree and Serpent worship which in ancient times prevailed so extensively over the East. The serpent was formerly regarded as the symbol of a beneficent God. In Hindustan, says Maurice, "the veneration of the serpent is evident in every page of their mythologic history, in which every fabulous personage of note is represented as grasping or as environed with a serpent." According to Lajard, the word which signifies "life" in the greater part of the Semitic languages signifies also "a serpent" And Jacob Bryant says that the word "Ab," which in Hebrew means Father, has also the same meaning as the Egyptian "Ob," or "Aub," and signifies "a serpent," thus etymologically uniting the two ideas. The Tree and the Serpent were frequently associated, although they were sometimes worshipped apart. The Aryan races of the Western world mostly worshipped the Tree alone. The Scandinavians had their great ash "Yggdrasill," whose triple root reaches to the depths of the universe, while its majestic stem overtops the heavens and its branches fill the world. The Grecian oracles were delivered from the oak of Dodona, and the priests set forth their decrees on its leaves. Nutpi or Neith, the goddess of divine life, was by the Egyptians represented as seated among the branches of the Tree of Life, in the paradise of Osiris. The "Hom," the sacred tree of the Persians, is spoken of in the Zendavesta as the "Word of Life," and, when consecrated, was partaken of as a sacrament. An oak was the sacred tree of the ancient Druids of Britain. We inherit their custom of gathering the sacred mistletoe at Yule-tide, while in our Christmas Tree we have a remnant of the old Norse tree-worship. During the Middle Ages the worship of trees was forbidden in France by the ecclesiastical councils, and in England by the laws of Canute. A learned antiquary remarks that "the English maypole decked with colored rags and tinsel, and the merry morice-dancers (the gaily decorated May sweeps) with the mysterious and now almost defunct personage, Jack-in-the-green, are all but worn-out remnants of the adoration of gods in trees that once were sacred in England."

Now the serpent and the tree were originally both symbolic of the generative powers of nature, and they were interchangeable. Sometimes one was employed, sometimes the other, and sometimes both. But in that great religious reformation which took place in the faiths of the ancient world about 600 years before the time of Christ, the serpent was degraded, and made to stand as a symbol of Ahriman, the god of evil, who, in the Persic religion, waged incessant war against Ormuzd, the god of beneficence. The Persian myth of the Fall is thus rendered from the Zendavesta by Kalisch:—

"The first couple, the parents of the human race, Meshia and Meshiane, lived originally in purity and innocence. Perpetual happiness was promised them by Ormuzd, the creator of every good gift, if they persevered in their virtue. But an evil demon (Dev) was sent to them by Ahriman, the representative of everything noxious and sinful. He appeared unexpectedly in the form of a serpent, and gave them the fruit of a wonderful tree, Hom, which imparted immortality and had the power of restoring the dead to life. Thus evil inclinations entered their hearts; all their moral excellence was destroyed. Ahriman himself appeared wider the form of the same reptile, and completed the work of seduction. They acknowledged him instead of Ormuzd as the creator of everything good; and the consequence was they forfeited for ever the eternal happiness for which they were destined."

Every reader will at once perceive how similar this is to the Hebrew story of the Fall. The similarity is intelligible when we remember that all the literature of the ancient Jews was put into its present form by the learned scribes who returned with the remnant of the people from the Babylonish captivity, and who were full of the ideas that obtained in the Persian religion as reformed by the traditional Zoroaster.

As we have said, the Hebrew story of the Fall contains clear relics of Tree and Serpent worship. There is also abundant proof that during the long ages in which the Jews oscillated between polytheism and monotheism this worship largely prevailed. Even up to the reign of Hezekiah, as we find in the Second Book of Kings, the serpent was worshipped in groves, to the great anger of the king, who cast out the idolatry from among his people.

Having explained the subject thus, let us now assume with orthodox Christians that the serpent in Eden was animated by the Devil, or was indeed the Devil himself incarnate.

We have already observed that the Devil excels his three rivals in wisdom and in power. While they were toiling so strenuously to create the world and all that therein is, he quietly stood or sat by as a spectator. "All right," he might have murmured, "work away as hard as you please. You've more strength than sense. My turn will soon come. When the job is finished we shall see to whom all this belongs." When the work was completed and they had pronounced all things good, in stepped the Devil, and in the twinkling of an eye rendered imperfect all that they had so labored to create perfect;'turning everything topsy-turvey, seducing the first pair of human beings, sowing the seeds of original sin, and at one stroke securing the wholesale damnation of our race. What were they about, to let him do all this with such consummate ease? Surely they must have slept like logs, and thus left the whole game in his hands. He made himself the "prince of this world," although they created it; and if those may laugh who win, he was entitled to roar out his mirth to the shaking of the spheres.

Besides being the prince of this world and of the powers of darkness, the Devil is described as the father of lies. This, however, is a gross libel on his character. Throughout the contest with his rivals he played with perfect fairness. And from Genesis to Revelation there can be adduced no single instance in which he departs from the strict line of truth. On one occasion when Jehovah desired a lying spirit to go forth and prophesy falsely to his people, he found one ready to his hand in heaven and had no need to trouble Satan for a messenger. The Lord God had told Adam, "Of the tree of knowledge of good and evil, thow shalt not eat of it; for in the day that thou eatest thereof thow shalt surely die." Nay, said the Devil, when he began business "ye shall not surely die; for God doth know that in the day ye eat thereof, then your eyes shall be opened, and ye shall be as gods, knowing good and evil." Every word of his speech was true. Instead of dying "in the day" that he ate of the fruit Adam lived to the fine old age of nine hundred and thirty years.

And after the "fall" the Lord God said, "Behold, the man is become as one of us, to know good and evil." The Devil's truthfulness is thus amply vindicated.

Satan's visit to Eve was paid in the form of a serpent. She manifested no astonishment at being accosted by such a creature. It may be that the whole menagerie of Eden spoke in the human tongue, and that Balaam's ass was only what the biologists would call "a case of reversion" to the primitive type. Josephus and most of the Fathers conceived of the serpent as having had originally a human voice and legs; so that if he could not have walked about with Eve arm in arm, he might at least have accompanied her in a dance. Milton, however, discredits the legs, and represents the serpent thus:

> "Not with indented wave,
> Prone on the ground, as since, but on his rear,
> Circular base of rising folds, that towered,
> Fold above fold, a surging maze, his head
> Crested aloft, and carbuncle his eyes;
> With burnish'd neck of verdant gold, erect
> Amidst his circling spires, that on the grass
> Floated redundant."

Very splendid! But the doctors differ, and who shall decide? What followed the eating of the forbidden fruit we have dealt with in "Eve and the Apple." We shall therefore at once come to the curse pronounced upon the serpent "And the Lord God said unto the serpent, Because thou hast done this, thou art cursed above all cattle, and above every beast of the field; upon thy belly shalt thou go, and dust shalt thou eat all the days of thy life: and I will put enmity between thee and the woman, and between thy seed and her seed; it shall bruise thy head, and thou shalt bruise his heel."

The final portion of this curse is flagrantly mythological Among the Hindoos, Krishna also, as the incarnation of Vishnu, is represented now as treading on the bruised head of a conquered serpent, and now as entwined by it, and stung in the heel. In Egyptian pictures and sculptures, likewise, the serpent is seen pierced through the head by the spear of the goddess Isis. The "enmity" between mankind and the serpent is, however, not universal Amongst the Zulus the snake is held in great veneration, as their dead ancestors are supposed to reappear in that form; and in ancient times, as we have already observed, serpents were actually worshipped.

The middle portion of the curse has not yet been fulfilled. The serpent lives on more nutritious food than dust. In the Zoological Gardens the inmates of the serpent-house enjoy a more solid diet The fact is, we have here an oriental superstition. Kalisch points out that "the great scantiness of food? on which the serpent can subsist, gave rise to the belief, entertained by many Eastern nations, that they eat dust." This belief is referred to in Micah vii, 17, Isaiah lxv., 25, and elsewhere in the Bible. Among the Indians the serpent is believed to live on wind.

That the serpent "goes" upon its "belly" is, of course, a fact. Before the curse it must have moved about in some other way. Milton's poetical solution of the difficulty we have already given. During the Middle Ages those seraphic doctors of theology, who gravely argued how many angels could dance on the point of a needle, speculated also on the serpent's method of locomotion before the "fall." Some thought the animal had legs, some that it undulated gracefully on its back, and others that it hopped about on its tail. The ever bold Delitzsch decides that "its mode of motion and its form were changed," but closes the controversy by adding, "of the original condition of the serpent it is, certainly, impossible to frame to ourselves a conjecture." All this is mere moonshine. Geology, as Colenso remarks, shows us that the serpent was the same kind of creature as it is now, in the ages long before man existed on the earth.

Why the serpent was cursed at all is a question which no Christian can answer. The poor animal was seized, mastered, occupied, and employed by the Devil, and was therefore absolutely irresponsible for what occurred. It had committed no offence, and consequently the curse upon it, according to Christian doctrine, was a most brutal and wanton outrage.

Having done such a splendid stroke of business in Eden, the Devil retired, quite satisfied that the direction he had given to the affairs of this world was so strong and certain as to obviate the necessity of his personal supervision. Fifteen centuries later the human race had grown so corrupt that God (that is, the three persons in one) resolved to drown them all; preserving, however, eight live specimens to repeople the world. How the Devil must have laughed again! He knew that Noah and his family possessed the seeds of original sin, which they would assuredly transmit to their children, and thus prolong the corruption through all time. Short-sighted as ever, Jehovah refrained from completing the devastation, after which he might have started afresh. So sure was the Devil's grip on God's creation that, a few centuries after the Flood, there were not found ten righteous men in the whole city of Sodom, and no doubt other cities were almost as bad.

According to the Bible, the Devil's long spell of rest was broken in the reign of King David, the man after God's own heart, but a very great scoundrel nevertheless. The Second Book of Samuel (xxiv., 1) tells us that "Again the anger of the Lord was kindled against Israel, and he moved David against them to say, Go, number Israel and Judah." Now the First Book of Chronicles (xxi, 1) in relating the same incident says, "And Satan stood up against Israel, and provoked David to number Israel" Who shall reconcile this discrepancy? Was it God, was it Satan, or was it both? Imagine David with the celestial and infernal powers whispering the same counsel into either ear! A Scotch minister once told us that this difficulty was only apparent. The Devil, said he, exercises only a delegated power, and acts only by the express or tacit permission of

God; so that it matters not which is said to have provoked David. Yes, but what of the consequences? Because the king, despite all protests, took a census of his people, the Lord sent a destroying angel, who slew by pestilence seventy thousand of them. Where, in the whole history of religion, shall we find a viler sample of divine injustice?

Besides, if the Devil acts in all cases only by God's permission, the latter is responsible for all the former's wrongdoing. The principal, and not the agent, must bear the guilt. And this suggests a curious problem. Readers of "Robinson Crusoe" will remember that when Man Friday was undergoing a course of theological instruction, he puzzled his master by asking why God did not convert the Devil. To his unsophisticated mind it was plain that the conversion of the Devil would annihilate sin. Robinson Crusoe changed the subject to avoid looking foolish, but Man Friday's question remains in full force. Why does not God convert the Devil? The great Thomas Aquinas is reported to have prayed for the Devil's conversion through a whole long night. Robert Burns concludes his "Address to the Deil" with a wish that he "wad tak a thought an' men'." And Sterne, in one of his wonderful strokes of pathos, makes Corporal Trim say of the Devil, "He is damned already, your honor;" whereupon, "I am sorry for it," quoth Uncle Toby. Why, oh why, we repeat, does not God convert the Devil, and thus put a stop for ever to the damnation of mankind? Why do not the clergy pray without cease for that one object? Because they dare not. The Devil is their best friend. Abolish him, and disestablish hell, and their occupation would be gone. They must stick to their dear Devil, as their most precious possession, their stock-in-trade, their talisman of power, without whom they were worse than nothing.

The Devil's adventures in the Book of Job are very amusing. One day there was a drawing-room or levée held in heaven. The sons of God attended, and Satan came also among them. He seems to have so closely resembled the rest of the company that only God detected the difference. This is not surprising, for the world has seen some very godly sons of God, so very much like the Devil, that if he met one of them in a dark lane by night, he might almost suspect it to be his own ghost. God, who knows everything, as usual asked a number of questions. Where had Satan been, and what had he been doing? Satan replied, like a gentleman of independent means, that he had been going to and fro in the earth, and walking up and down in it. "Well," said the Lord, "have you observed my servant Job? What a good man! perfect and upright I'm proud of him." Oh yes, Satan had observed him. He keeps a sharp eye on all men. As old Bishop Latimer said, whatever parson is out of his parish the Devil is always in his. "Doth Job fear God for nought?" said Satan. "He is wealthy, prosperous, happy, and respected; you fence him about from evil; but just let trouble come upon him, and he will curse thee to thy face." This was a new view of the subject; the Lord had never seen it in this light before. So he determined to make an experiment. With God's sanction Satan went forth to afflict Job. He despoiled his substance, slaughtered his children, covered him with sore boils from head to foot, and then set on his wife to "nag" him. But Job triumphed; he did not curse God, and thus Satan was foiled. Subsequently Job became richer than ever and more renowned, while a fresh family grew up around his knees. "So," say the Christians, "all's well that ends well!" Not so, however; for there remains uneffaced the murder of Job's children, who were hurriedly despatched out of the world in the very midst of their festivity. When the celestial and infernal powers play at conundrums, it is a great pity that they do not solve them up above or down below, and leave the poor denizens of this world free from the havoc of their contention.

In the New Testament, as in the Old, the Devil appears early on the scene. After his baptism in Jordan, Jesus was "led up of the spirit in the wilderness to be tempted of the Devil." When he had fasted forty days and nights he "was afterward hungered." Doctor Tanner overlooked this. The hunger of Jesus only began on the forty-first day. The Devil requests Jesus to change the stones into bread, but he declines to do so. Then he sets him "on a pinnacle of the temple" in Jerusalem, and desires him to throw himself down. Jesus must have been exceedingly sharp set in that position. Meanwhile, where was the Devil posted? He could scarcely have craned his neck up so as to hold a confabulation with Jesus from the streets, and we must therefore suppose that he was sharp set on another pinnacle. A pretty sight they must have been for the Jews down below! That temptation failing, the Devil takes Jesus "up into an exceeding high mountain, and showeth him all the kingdoms of the world, and the glory of them." This is remarkably like seeing round a corner, for however high we go we cannot possibly see the whole surface of a globe at once. "All these things," says Satan, "will I give thee if thou wilt fall down and worship me." What a generous Devil! They already belonged to Jesus, for doth not Scripture say the earth is the Lord's and the fulness thereof?—a text which should now read "the earth is the landlords' and the emptiness thereof." This temptation also fails, and the Devil retires in disgust.

What a pretty farce! Our burlesques and pantomimes are nothing to it. Satan knew Jesus, and Jesus knew Satan. Jesus knew that Satan would tempt him, and Satan knew that Jesus knew it. Jesus knew that Satan could not succeed, and Satan knew so too. Yet they kept the farce up night and day, for no one knows how long; and our great Milton in his "Paradise Regained" represents this precious pair arguing all day long, Satan retiring after sunset, and Jesus lying down hungry, cold and wet, and rising in the morning with damp clothes to renew the discussion.

Soon after Jesus went into the country of the Gergesenes, where he met two fierce men possessed with devils whom he determined to exorcise, The devils (for the Devil had grown numerous by then), not liking to be turned adrift on the world, without home or shelter, besought Jesus to let them enter the bodies of an herd of swine feeding by. This he graciously permitted. The devils left the men and entered the swine; whereupon the poor pigs, experiencing a novel sensation, never having had devils inside them before, "ran violently down a steep place into the sea, and perished in the waters." Whether the devils were drowned with the pigs this veracious history saith not. But the pigs themselves were not paid for. Jesus wrought the miracle at other people's expense. And the inhabitants of that part took precisely this view of the case. For "the whole city came out to meet Jesus: and when they saw him, they besought him that he would depart out of their coasts." No doubt they reflected that if he remained working miracles of that kind, at the end of a week not a single pig would be left alive in the district. Entering in Genesis, the Devil appropriately makes his exit in Revelation. The twelfth chapter of that holy nightmare describes him as "a great red dragon, having seven heads, and ten horns, and seven crowns upon his heads; and his tail drew the third part of the stars of heaven, and did cast them to the earth." What a tail! The writer's ideas of size were very chaotic. Bringing a third part of the stars of heaven to this earth, is much like trying to lodge a few thousand cannon-balls on the surface of a bullet.

Finally the Devil is to be "bound for a thousand years" in hell. Let us hope the chain will be strong; for if it should break, the pit has no bottom, and the Devil would go right through, coming out on the other side to renew his old tricks.

Such is the Romance of the Bible Devil. Was ever a more ludicrous story palmed off on a credulous world? The very clergy are growing ashamed of it. But there it is, inextricably interwoven with the rest of the "sacred" narrative, so that no skill can remove it without destroying the whole fabric. The Devil has been the Church's best friend, but he is doomed, and as their fraternal bond cannot be broken, he will drag it down to irretrievable perdition.

THE TEN PLAGUES
Or HOW MOSES HARRIED EGYPT

If a man who had never read the Bible before wished to amuse himself during a spare hour among its pages, we should recommend him to try the first fourteen chapters of Exodus. A more entertaining narrative was never penned. Even the fascinating Arabian Nights affords nothing better, provided we read it with the eyes of common sense, and without that prejudice which so often blinds us to the absurdities of "God's Word." At the end of the fourteenth chapter aforesaid, let the book be closed, and then let the reader ask himself whether he ever met with a more comical story. We have no doubt as to his answer; and we feel assured that he will agree with the poet Cowper in thinking that God does "move in a mysterious way his wonders to perform." Two hundred and fifteen years after the arrival of Israel in Egypt, God's chosen people had fallen into slavery. Yet they were exceedingly prolific, so that "the land was filled with them." Afraid of their growing numbers, Pharaoh "spake to the Hebrew midwives" and told them to kill all their male children at birth and leave only the daughters alive. This injunction the midwives very, properly disobeyed, excusing themselves on the ground that "the Hebrew women were lively and were delivered ere the midwives came in unto them." Had they obeyed Pharaoh, the Jewish race would have been extinguished, and Judaism and Christianity been never heard of.

But the comical fact as to these midwives is that there were only two of them, Shiphrah and Puah. What a busy pair they must have been! What patterns of ubiquitous industry! When the Jews quitted Egypt soon after they mustered six hundred thousand men, besides women and children. Now, supposing all these were collected together in one city, its size would equal that of London. How could two midwives possibly attend to all the confinements among such a population? And how much more difficult would their task be if the population were scattered over a wide area, as was undoubtedly the case with the Jews! Words fail us to praise the miraculous activity of these two ladies. Like the peace of God, it passes all understanding.

One of the male children born under the iron rule of Pharaoh was Moses, the son of Amram and Jochebed. The incidents of his eventful life will be fully recorded in our series of "Bible Heroes." Suffice it here to say that he was adopted and brought up by Pharaoh's daughter; that he became skilled in all the learning of the Egyptians; that he privily slew an Egyptian who had maltreated a Hebrew, and was obliged therefore to flee to the land of Midian, where he married Zipporah, a daughter of Jethro the priest. At this time Moses was getting on to his eightieth year. Now-a-days a man of that age sees only the grave before him, and has pretty nearly closed his account with the world. But in those days it was different. At the age of eighty Moses was just beginning his career. He was indeed a very astonishing old boy.

One day Moses was keeping his father-in-law's flock near Mount Horeb, when lo! a strange vision greeted his eyes. The "angel of the Lord appeared unto him in a flame of fire out of the midst of a bush," which burned without consuming. By "angel" we are to understand a vision or appearance only, for the being within the bush was God Almighty himself; and throughout the rest of the narrative the word "angel" is entirely dropped, only Lord or God being used. Moses approached this wonderful sight; but the Lord called out to him, "Draw not nigh hither: put off thy shoes from off thy feet, for the place whereon thou standest is holy ground." Thereupon Moses hid his face "for he was afraid to look upon God." Could anything be more ludicrous! Fancy God, the infinite spirit of the universe, secreting himself in a bush and setting it on fire, just to make a little display for the benefit of Moses! Our wonder, however, is presently lessened; for this God turns out to be only Jehovah "the Lord God of the Hebrews," a mere local deity, who cared only for his own people, and was quite ready to slaughter any number of the inhabitants of adjacent countries, besides being bitterly jealous of their gods. The utmost claimed for him is that he is the biggest God extant, and quite capable of thrashing all the other gods with one hand tied behind his back. He had heard the cries of his people and had determined to rescue them from bondage. He had also resolved to give Pharaoh and the Egyptians a taste of his quality, so that they might be forced to-admit his superiority to their gods. "I will let them know," said he to Moses, "who I am, and you shall be my agent. We'll confound their impudence before we've done with them. But don't let us be in a hurry, for the little drama I have devised requires a good deal of time. You go to Egypt and ask Pharaoh to let my people go. But don't suppose he will consent. That wouldn't suit my plans at all. I have decided to set you two playing at the little game of 'pull Moses, pull Pharaoh,' and I shall harden his heart against your demands so that there may be a fierce tussle. But don't be afraid. I am on your side, and just at the end of the game I'll join in and pull Pharaoh clean over. And mind you tell him all along that it is my power and not yours which works all the wonders I mean you to perform, for you are only my instrument, and I want all the glory myself. Play fair, Moses, play fair!" Moses was not unwilling to engage in this enterprise, but like a prudent Jew he required certain assurances of success. He therefore first raised an objection as to his own insignificance—"Who am I, that I should go unto Pharaoh?" To which God replied, "Certainly I will be with thee; and this shall be a token unto thee, that I have sent thee: When thou hast brought forth the people out of Egypt, ye shall serve God upon this mountain." Moses, however, required a much less remote token than this; so he again objected that nobody would believe him. Thereupon the Lord bade him cast his rod on the ground, and lo! it became a serpent Moses very naturally fled before it, till the Lord told him not to run away but to take it by the tail. He did so, and it became again a rod in his hand. Then the Lord bade him put his hand in his bosom, and on taking it out he found it was "leprous as snow." Again he put it in his bosom, and when he plucked it out it was once more sound and well. "There," said the Lord, "those signs will do in Egypt. When you evince them nobody will doubt you." Still hesitant,

Moses objected that he was very slow of speech. So he frankly desired the Lord to send someone else. No wonder the Lord grew angry at this persistent reluctance; nevertheless he restrained himself, and informed Moses that his brother Aaron, who was a good speaker, should accompany him. The prudent prophet seems to have been at length satisfied. At any rate he made no further objection, but after a little further conversation with the Lord, who was very talkative, he set forth on his journey to Egypt.

Singular to relate, the Lord met Moses at an inn on the road, and, instead of wishing him good-speed, sought to kill him. What a strange God, to be sure! Why did he want to kill his own messenger? And why, if he wanted to kill him, did he not succeed in doing it? Truly the ways of God are past finding out. The only reason discoverable for this queer conduct is that Moses' boy was uncircumcised. Zipporah, his wife, took a sharp stone and performed the rite of circumcision herself, casting the amputated morsel at the feet of the boy's father, with the remark that he was "a bloody husband." The Lord's anger was thereby appeased, and the text naively says that he then let Moses go.

Prompted by the Lord, Aaron went out into the wilderness to meet Moses, and they soon appeared together before "all the elders of the children of Israel," who readily believed in their mission when they heard Aaron's account of the Lord's conversation with Moses, and saw the wonderful signs. Afterwards the two brothers visited Pharaoh, but God had hardened his heart; so he denied all knowledge of the Lord, and refused to let Israel go. On the contrary, he commanded the taskmaskers to be even more rigorous with them, and, instead of giving them straw to make bricks, as theretofore, to make them gather straw for themselves. And when they complained, Pharaoh replied that they were an idle lot, and only wanted to go out and sacrifice to the Lord in order to avoid work. Whereupon they remonstrated with Moses for his interference, and he, in turn, remonstrated with God in very plain and disrespectful language. "Nonsense!" said the Lord, "now you shall see what I will do to Pharaoh."

Again Pharaoh was visited by the two brothers, who this time commenced to work the miracle. Aaron cast down his rod, and it became a serpent. But the magicians of Egypt, who were present by invitation of the King, were in nowise astonished. "Oh," said they, "is that all you can do?" Saying which, every man of them threw down his rod, and it also became a serpent. That was indeed an age of miracles! The magicians of Egypt wrought this wonder without any help from the Lord, and solely "with their enchantments." Here, then, was a pretty fix! So far, neither side had any advantage. Presently, however, Aaron's serpent—which thus proved itself a truly Jewish one—created a diversion by swallowing all the others up. We must suppose that it afterwards disgorged them, or else that Aaron's, rod was exceedingly stout when he got it back.

Pharaoh's heart remained obdurate, notwithstanding this sign, and he still refused to let the people go. And then the plagues commenced.

The first was a plague of blood. Aaron stretched forth his rod, and all the waters of Egypt, the streams, the rivers, the ponds, and the pools became blood. Even the water in vessels of stone and wood was ensanguined. The fish all died, and the river stank; and "there was blood throughout all the land of Egypt." This was a good start, but the magicians of Egypt beat it hollow; for, after Aaron had turned all the water of Egypt into blood, they turned the rest into blood. No wonder that Pharaoh's heart remained hardened! He quietly walked into his house and let the subject drop.

Seven days later Moses went again to Pharaoh and said, "Thus saith the Lord, let my people go." And Pharaoh said, "I won't." "Won't you?" answered Moses, "we shall see." Forthwith Aaron stretched forth his rod over the streams, rivers, and ponds, and brought on the second plague in the shape of frogs, which swarmed all over the land. They entered the houses, penetrated to the bedrooms, mounted the beds, slipped into the kneading-troughs, and even got into the ovens, although one would expect frogs to give such hot places a very wide berth. What a squelching of frogs there must have been! The Egyptians could not have stood absolutely still, and the land was covered with them. Still unfoiled, the magicians, "with their enchantments, followed suit, and brought up frogs too." Yet, as the land was already covered with frogs, it is difficult to see how the new comers found room, unless they got on the backs of the others, and went hopping about in couples. Pharaoh now relented. He called for Moses, and said, "Intreat your Lord to take away these nasty frogs, and I will let the people go." "That will I," said Moses, "and you shall know that there is none like unto the Lord our God." The next day the frogs died out of the houses, villages, and fields, and were gathered into heaps, so that again "the land stank." But when Pharaoh saw that there was respite, he hardened his heart again, "as the Lord had said."

The third act of this tragi-comedy was decisive in one sense, for in it the magicians of Egypt were obliged to retire from the competition. Aaron stretched forth his rod again and smote the dust of the earth, all of which instantly became lice, in man and in beast. Before this dirty miracle the magicians of Egypt shrank dismayed. They made a feeble and altogether unsuccessful attempt to imitate Aaron's performance, and then drew back, declining to continue the contest. The lice settled them. "This," said they, "is the finger of God." But Pharaoh still refused to knuckle under. Even against the force of this supreme wonder his heart was steeled.

So the fourth plague came. A grievous swarm of flies descended on Egypt, so that "the land was corrupted by reason of them. But not a single fly crossed over into the land of Goshe" where the Jews dwelt. Thereupon Pharaoh called for Moses and Aaron, and told them he was willing to let their people go and sacrifice to the Lord for three days, but not outside Egypt. Moses reiterated his demand for a three days' journey into the wilderness. Whereto Pharaoh replied that they might go, but "not too far." Moses then undertook to banish the flies. And he was as good as his word; for there was made such a clean sweep of them that "not one remained." This precious narrative always runs to extremes. Egypt without a fly in it would be in a very abnormal condition. At ordinary times the land is infested with flies; so much so, indeed, that large numbers of the people suffer from diseased eyes, in consequence of these insects incessantly fastening on the sores caused by the irritating sand which fills the air. It was absurd for this Hebrew story-teller to scotch the last fly; he should have left sufficient to maintain the character of the country.

Again Pharaoh's heart was hardened, and when the flies were banished he refused to "let the people go." So the fifth plague came. A "very grievous murrain," which spared the cattle of Israel, broke out on the cattle of Egypt, and with such virulence that they all died. Pharaoh found on inquiry that there was "not one of the cattle of the Israelites dead," yet for all that his heart was hardened, and he would not let the people go.

So the sixth plague came. Aaron took "handfuls of ashes of the furnace," which Moses sprinkled towards heaven, and "it became a boil breaking forth with blains upon man and upon beast." Even the magicians were afflicted. Now the readers will bear in mind that all the cattle of Egypt were killed by the fifth, plague. What beasts, then, were these tortured with boils? Were they dead carcasses, or were they live cattle miraculously created in the interim? Surely this is a thing which "no fellah can understand." From the serpent of Eden to Jonah's whale, the animals of the Bible are a queer lot.

Pharaoh's heart remaining still hardened, God commanded Moses to make a special appeal to him, and to get up early in the morning for that purpose. So Moses stood before Pharaoh and said, "Thus saith the Lord God of the Hebrews, let my people go, that they may serve me. If you refuse I shall plague you and your people worse than ever, and so teach you that there is none like me in all the earth. Don't puff yourself up with conceit, for you were made what you are only in order that through you my power might be manifested. You had better cave in at once." But Pharaoh would not harken. He tacitly declared that the Lord God of the Hebrews might go to Jericho.

So the seventh plague came. A fierce hail, accompanied by fire that ran along the ground, smote all that was in the field, both man and beast. It smote also every herb of the field and brake every tree of the field. Only those were saved who "feared the Lord" and stayed in doors with their servants and cattle. Fortunately the wheat and the rice were spared, as they were not grown up; or there would have been a famine in Egypt compared with which the seven years of scarcity in Joseph's time had sunk into insignificance. Pharaoh now relented and repented. "I have sinned this time," he said, "the Lord is righteous, and I and my people are wicked." And Moses, seeing that the king had recognised Jehovah as the true cock of the theological walk, procured a cessation of the thunder and the hail. But lo! when Pharaoh perceived this, he hardened his heart again, and "sinned yet more." The obduracy of this potentate, under the manipulation of God, is really becoming monotonous. So the eighth plague came. After a day and a night of east wind, a prodigious swarm of locusts went up over the land of Egypt, covering the face of the whole earth, and darkening the ground. They "did eat every herb of the land, and all the fruit of the trees which the hail had spared." But we were told that the hail smote every herb, and brake every tree. What then was left for the locusts to eat? The writer of this narrative had a very short memory, or else a stupendous power of belief.

Again Pharaoh confessed that he had sinned. The locusts were cleared away, and so effectually that "not one remained." But "the Lord hardened Pharaoh's heart" for the eighth time, and he refused to let the people go. Whereupon Moses brought darkness over the land of Egypt, a thick darkness that might be felt. This thick darkness lasted in Egypt for three days, during which time the people "saw not one another, neither rose any from his place." We presume, therefore, that they all starved for that time. Poor devils! What had they done to be treated thus? All the children of Israel, however, had light in their dwellings. Why then did they not avail themselves of such a fine opportunity to escape? It was a splendid chance, yet they let it slip. Perhaps Moses did not give the word, and they were like a flock of sheep without him. Perhaps they wished to stay and see the rest of the fun. For more was coming, although it was anything but fun to the poor Egyptians.

To them indeed it was an awful tragedy such as we lack words to describe. Moses commanded the Jews to take a male lamb for each household, to kill it, and to daub its blood over the two side-posts and on the upper door-posts of their houses. The flesh they were to eat in the night, roasted, with bitter herbs and unleavened bread, as the inauguration of the Passover. The Lord meant to pass through the land in the dark, and slay all the firstborn in Egypt; and lest he should make some mistakes he required the Jews' houses to be marked with blood so that he might distinguish them. We should expect God to dispense with such "aids to memory." What followed must be told in the language of Scripture: "At midnight the Lord smote all the firstborn in the land of Egypt, from the firstborn of Pharaoh that sat on the throne unto the firstborn of the captive that was in the dungeon; and all the firstborn of cattle. And Pharaoh rose up in the night, he, and all his servants, and all the Egyptians; and there was a great cry in Egypt; for there was not a house where there was not one dead." The reader's imagination will picture the horror of this scene. That "great cry in Egypt" arose from a people who were the first victims of God's hatred of all who stood in the way of his chosen "set of leprous slaves." And in this case the tragedy was the more awful, and the more inexcusably atrocious, because God deliberately planned it. He could easily have softened Pharaoh's heart, but he chose to harden it. He could have brought his people out of Egypt in peace, but he preferred that they should start amidst wailings of agony, and leave behind them a track of blood.

Yet in the tragedy there is a touch of comedy. Those beasts that were first killed by the murrian and afterwards plagued by the boil, at last lose their firstborn by the tenth plague. Besides, there is a touch of the ludicrous in the statement that every house had one dead. All the firstborn of such a large population could not have been present at that time. Some might have left Egypt for purposes of trade, and others would certainly have been cut off before by death. The story of the tenth plague, like the other nine, requires to be taken with a very large grain of salt.

Pharaoh and the Egyptians were now anxious to get rid of the Jews. So God's people departed in haste. They took good care, however, not to go empty-handed. They "borrowed" of the Egyptians, without the remotest intention of ever paying them back, jewels of silver, jewels of gold, and raiment. In fact they "spoiled the Egyptians." In recent times the modern Egyptians have wiped off that old score by spoiling a few Jewish moneylenders, and so returned tit for tat.

God led his people past instead of through the land of the Philistines, lest they should be frightened by war, and wish to return to Egypt. He does not seem to have known their character. Considering the delight with which they subsequently warred against their enemies, and the joy they took in wholesale massacre, we are inclined to think that they would have just liked to get their hands into the business of fighting by trying conclusions with the Philistines. Moses carried off the bones of Joseph, which must have been rather stale by that time. And God went before the huge host of six hundred thousand men on foot, besides women and children, and a mixed multitude of followers; by day in a pillar of cloud, to lead them the way, and by night in a pillar of fire, to give them light, until at length they found themselves encamped before the Red Sea.

In the meanwhile God had again hardened Pharaoh's heart, for the express purpose of killing some more Egyptians and getting more honor to himself. The Israelites soon heard that Pharaoh was pursuing them with an army, and they remembered his dreadful war chariots. They found themselves literally between the devil and the deep sea. Whereupon they murmured against Moses for bringing them out into the wilderness to die. But he, disregarding them, stretched forth his miraculous rod over the sea, and lo! the waters parted, forming a wall on either side of a safe passage, through which the Jews travelled with dry feet. Pharaoh and his host, however, attempting the same feat, were overwhelmed by the down-rushing sea-ramparts, and all drowned. There remained, says Exodus, not so much as one of them.

We have heard a different account of this affair. A negro preacher once explained that the Red Sea, just at that time, was "a little bit frozen over," and the Jews, carrying only what they had borrowed "frum the Gyptians," crossed the ice safely; but when Pharaoh came with his thundering war-chariots, the ice broke, and "dey all was drown'd." But a nigger in the audience objected that the Red Sea is "in de quator," and is never frozen over. "War did you larn dat?" asked the preacher. "In de jografy," was the reply. "Ah," was the ready retort, "dat's war you made de mistake; dis was a very long time ago, and dere was no jografy and no quator den." That nigger preacher's explanation seems quite as good as the one given by "Moses."

We leave the Jews with their Lord God on the safe side of the Red Sea, where Moses heads the men in singing a joyful song of praise, and Miriam the prophetess heads the women with timbrel and with dance. Jehovah has ended his plaguing of the Egyptians, after more than decimating them. He has covered his name with terrible splendour, and proved "that there is none like him" to a world which is very happy to be assured of the fact. Two such monsters would make earth a hell. Reader! did you ever meet with a more extraordinary story than this of the Ten Plagues? and can you regard the book which contains it as God's Word?

JONAH AND THE WHALE

We have often wondered whether Shakespeare had the story of Jonah in his mind when he wrote that brief dialogue between Hamlet and Polonius, which immediately precedes the famous closet-scene in the Master's greatest play—

Hamlet.—Do you see yonder cloud that's almost in shape of a camel?

> *Polonius.—By the mass, and 'tis like a camel, indeed.*
> *Hamlet.—Methinks it is like a weasel.*
> *Polonius.—It is backed like a weasel.*
> *Hamlet.—Or like a whale?*
> *Polonius.—Very like a whale.*

Having, however, no means whereby to decide this question, we must content ourselves with broaching it, and leave the reader to form his own conclusion. Yet we cannot refrain from expressing our opinion that the story of the strange adventures of the prophet Jonah is "very like a whale."

In another of Shakespeare's plays, namely "The Tempest," we find a phrase which exactly applies to the romance of Jonah. When Trinculo discovers Caliban lying on the ground, he proceeds to investigate the monster. "What," quoth he, "have we here? a man or a fish? dead or alive? A fish: he smells like a fish; a very ancient and fish-like smell." Now that is a most admirable description of the Book of Jonah. It has "a very ancient and fish-like smell." In fact, it is about the fishiest of all the fishy stories ever told.

Sailors' "yarns" have become proverbial for their audacious and delicious disregard of truth, and the Book of Jonah is "briny" from beginning to end. It contains only forty-eight verses, but its brevity is no defect. On the contrary, that is one of its greatest charms. The mind takes in the whole story at once, and enjoys it undiluted; as it were a goblet of the fine generous wine of romance. Varying the expression, the Book of Jonah may be called the perfect cameo of Bible fiction.

When the Book of Jonah was written no one precisely knows, nor is it discoverable who wrote it. According to Matthew Arnold some unknown man of genius gave to Christendom the fourth gospel, and with sublime self-abnegation allowed his name to perish. A similar remark must be made concerning the unknown author who gave to the world this racy story of Jonah and the whale. We heartily wish his name had been preserved for remembrance and praise.

Our marginal Bibles date the Book of Jonah b.c. cir. 862. Other authorities give, the more recent date of b.c. 880 as that of the events recorded in it. This chronology will suggest an important reflection later on.

The wonderful story of Jonah and the whale begins in this wise:—
"Now the word of the Lord came unto Jonah, the son of Amittai, saying, Arise, go to Nineveh, that great city, and cry against it; for their wickedness is come up before me."

Who Amittai was, and whether man or woman, is a problem still unsolved; but it is reasonable to suppose the name was that of Jonah's father, as the ancient Jews paid no superfluous attentions to women, and generally traced descent from the paternal stem alone. Amittai belonged to a place called Gathhepher, "the village of the Cow's tail," or, as otherwise interpreted, "the Heifer's trough." Jonah's tomb is said to have been long shown on a rocky hill near the town; but whether the old gentleman was ever buried there no man can say. According to Mr. Bradlaugh, the word Jonah means a dove, and is by some derived from an Arabic root, signifying to be weak or gentle. Another interpretation, by Gesenius, is a feeble, gentle bird. This refractory prophet was singularly ill-named. If his cognomen was bestowed on him by his parents, they must have been greatly deceived as to his character. The proverb says that it is a wise son that knows his own father; and with the history of Jonah before us, we may add that it is a wise father who rightly knows his own son.

The solicitude of "the Lord God of the Hebrews" for the welfare of the Ninevites is to the sceptical mind an extraordinary phenomenon. It is one of the very few cases in which he shows the slightest concern for any other people than the Jews. His ordinary practice was to slaughter them wholesale by pestilence or the sword; and it is therefore very refreshing to meet with such an instance of his merciful care. For once he remembers that the rest of Adam's posterity are his children, and possess a claim on his attention.

Jonah, however, did not share this benign sentiment; and disrelishing the missionary enterprise assigned him, he "rose up to flee unto Tarshish from the presence of the Lord." Jehovah does not seem to have been omnipresent then; that attribute attaches to him only since the beginning of the Christian era, when he assumed universal sway. Long before the time of Jonah, another man, the first ever born in this world, namely Cain, also "went out from the presence of the Lord, and dwelt in the land of Nod;" probably so called because the Lord was not quite awake in that locality. No one knows were Nod was situated, nor can the most learned archaeologists denote the actual position of Tarshish. These two places would be well worth study. A careful examination of them would to some extent reveal what went on in those parts of the world to which God's presence did not extend; and we should be able to compare their geological and other records with those of the rest of the world. No doubt some striking differences would be perceptible.

Jonah determined to voyage by the Joppa and Tarshish line. So he went to the former port and embarked in one of the Company's ships, after paying his fare like a man.

Having a perfectly untroubled conscience, and no apprehension of his coming troubles, Jonah no doubt felt highly elated at having done the Lord so neatly. Perhaps it was this elation of spirits which safe-guarded him from sea-sickness. At any rate he went "down into the sides of the ship," and there slept the sleep of the just. So profound was his slumber, that it was "quite unbroken" by the horrible tempest that ensued. The Lord had his eye on Jonah, for the prophet had not yet reached the safe refuge of Tarshish; and he "sent out a great wind into the sea, and there was a mighty tempest in the sea, so that the ship was likely to be broken." The mariners "cast forth the wares that were in the ship" to lighten her, and toiled hard to keep afloat; but their efforts were apparently fruitless, and nothing lay before them but the certain prospect of a watery grave. The reader will be able to imagine the tumult of the scene; the dash of ravening waves, the fierce howling of the wind, the creaking of masts and the straining of cordage, the rolling and pitching of the good ship and the shifting of her cargo, the captain's hoarse shouts of command and the sailors' loud replies, alternated with frenzied appeals to their gods for help. Yet amidst all the uproar Jonah still slept, as though the vessel were gaily skimming the waters before a pleasant breeze.

Let us pause here to interpose a question. Did the "great wind sent out into the sea" by the Lord confine its attentions to the immediate vicinity of Jonah's ship, or did it cause a general tempest and perhaps send some other vessels to Davy Jones's locker? As no restrictions are mentioned, we presume that the tempest was general, and that the Lord's wind, like the Lord's rain referred to by Jesus, fell alike upon the just and the unjust. This circumstance very naturally heightens our previous conception of his righteousness.

That the Lord, or some other supernatural power, caused the tempest, the mariners of Jonah's ship and their captain never once doubted. Living as they did, and as we do not, under a miraculous dispensation, they attributed every unusual, and especially every unpleasant, occurrence to the agency of a god. The idea of predicting storms, with which the civilised world is now familiar, they would doubtless have regarded as blasphemous and absurd. It is, therefore, by no means wonderful that every man on board (except Jonah, who was fast asleep) "called unto his god." Ignorant of what god was afflicting them, they appealed impartially all round, in the hope of hitting the right one. But the circle of their deities did not include the one which sent the wind; so the tempest continued to prevail, despite their prayers.

In this extremity a happy thought occurred to the "ship-master." It struck him that the strange passenger down below might know something about the tempest, and that his god might have caused it. Forthwith there dawned within him a recollection of words which Jonah had uttered on embarking. Had he not told them "that he fled from the presence of the Lord?" "Dear me," the captain probably said to himself, "what a fool I was not to think of this before. That chap down below is the occasion of all these troubles; I'll go and hunt him up, confound him!" Thereupon he doubtless slapped his thigh, as is the wont of sailors when they solve a difficulty or hit on a brilliant idea; after which he descended "into the sides of the ship," whither Jonah had gone. There he found the prophet slumbering as peacefully as a weanling child, with a smile of satisfaction playing over his Hebrew features. We can imagine the captain's profound disgust in presence of this scene. He and his men had been toiling and praying, and, alas! pitching the cargo overboard, in order to save their skins; and all the while the occasion of their trouble had been lying fast asleep! Preserving an outward decorum, however, he accosted Jonah in very mild terms. "What meanest thou, O sleeper?" said he, "Arise, call upon thy God, if so be that God will think upon us, that we perish not."

What exquisite simplicity! It reminds us of the childlike and bland Sir Henry Drummond Wolff, when he opposed Mr. Brad-laugh's entry to the House of Commons. That honorable champion of Almighty God objected to Mr. Bradlaugh on the ground that he acknowledged no God, and was thus vastly different from the other members of the House, all of whom "believed in some kind of deity or other." You must have a god to be a legislator, it seems, even if that god is, as the Americans say, only a little tin Jesus. So the captain of this tempest-tost ship desired Jonah to call upon his god. He made no inquiry into the character of the god, any more than did Sir Henry Drummond Wolff on a later occasion. It was enough to know that Jonah had "some kind of deity or other." Any god would do.

Now comes the most remarkable episode in this wonderful story. The captain and the crew were aware that Jonah had "fled from the presence of the Lord," because he had told them; they had, therefore, every reason to believe that Jonah's god had caused the tempest. Yet, curiously enough, instead of at once proceeding on this belief, they said, everyone to his fellow, "Come, and let us cast lots, that we may know for whose cause this evil is upon us." This wholly superfluous procedure may, perhaps, be attributed to their exceptional love of justice. They wished to make assurance doubly sure before they "went for" Jonah. And with sweet simplicity they had recourse to the casting of lots, in which their wills would be inoperative, and the whole responsibility of deciding be thrown on the gods, who alone possessed the requisite information.

The lot of course fell upon Jonah. Any other result would have spoiled the story. "Then," continues our narrative, "said they unto him, Tell us, we pray thee, for whose cause this evil is upon us? What is thine occupation? and whence comest thou? what is thy country? and of what people art thou? And he said unto them, I am an Hebrew, and I fear the Lord, the God of heaven, which hath made the sea and the dry land. Then were the men exceedingly afraid, and said unto him, Why hast thou done this? For the men knew that he fled from the presence of the Lord, because he had told them. Then said they unto him, What shall we do unto thee, that the sea may be calm unto us? for the sea wrought and was tempestuous. And he said unto them, Take me up, and cast me forth into the sea; so shall the sea be calm unto you: for I know that for my sake this great tempest is upon you."

We are almost dumb with astonishment before this act of self-sacrifice on the part of Jonah, for which his previous history left us quite unprepared. Who would have thought him capable of such disinterested conduct? His self-abnegation was assuredly heroic, and may even be called sublime. No doubt the captain and crew of the ship were as much astonished as we are, and their opinion of Jonah went up several hundred per cent. They resolved to make a last supreme effort before turning him into a fish-bait. But all their gallant endeavors were discovered to be futile and a mere waste of time. So the men, more in sorrow than in anger, finally took Jonah up and threw him overboard. They had done their best for him, and now, finding that they could do no more except at too great a risk, they sadly left him to do the rest for himself.

Immediately, we are told, "the sea ceased from her raging." Jonah was oil upon the troubled waters. What an invaluable recipe does this furnish us against the dangers of the deep sea! The surest method of allaying a storm is to throw a prophet overboard. Every ship should carry a missionary in case of need. It would, indeed, be well if the law made this compulsory. The cost of maintaining the missionary would be more than covered by the saving effected in insurance. Here is a splendid field for Christian self-sacrifice! Hundreds of gentlemen who are now engaged in very doubtful labor among the heathen, might engage in this new enterprise with the absolute certainty of a beneficent result; for poor ungodly mariners would thus be spared a hasty dispatch from this world without time to repent and obtain forgiveness, and be allowed ample leisure to secure salvation.

When the men saw that "the sea ceased from her raging" on Jonah's being cast into her depths, "they feared the Lord exceedingly, and offered a sacrifice unto the Lord, and made vows." To the sceptical mind it would seem that they had much more reason to "fear" the Lord during the continuance of the tempest than after it had subsided. It also seems strange that they should have the means wherewith to offer a sacrifice. Perhaps they had a billy-goat on board, and made him do duty, in default of anything better. Or failing even a billy-goat, as the Lord God of the Hebrews could only be propitiated by the shedding of blood, they perhaps caught and immolated a stray rat. The nature of their "vows" is not recorded, but it is not unreasonable to assume that they swore never again to take on board a passenger fleeing "from the presence of the Lord."

Meanwhile, what had become of poor Jonah? Most men would be effectually settled if thrown overboard in a storm. But there are some people who were not born to be drowned, and Jonah was one of them. He was destined to another fate. The Lord, it appears, "had prepared a great fish to swallow up Jonah," and the feat was of course duly performed. Our narrative does not describe the character of this "great fish," but light is cast on the subject by another passage of Scripture. In the twelfth chapter of St. Matthew, and the fortieth verse, Jesus is represented as saying, "For as Jonas was three days and three nights in the whale's belly; so shall the Son of man be three days and three nights in the heart of the earth." The great fish was then a whale. Jesus said so, and there can be no higher authority. Sharks and such ravenous fish have an unpleasant habit of "chawing" their victims pretty considerably before swallowing them; so, on the whole, we prefer to believe that it was a whale. Yet the Levant is a curious place for a whale to be lurking in. The creature must have been miraculously led there to go through its appointed performance. It must also have been "prepared," to use the language of the Bible, in a very remarkable way, for the gullet of a whale is not large enough to allow of the passage of an object exceeding the size of an ordinary herring. Swallowing Jonah must have been a tough job after the utmost preparation. With a frightfully distended throat, however, the whale did its best, and by dint of hard striving at last got Jonah down.

Having properly taken Jonah in out of the wet, the poor whale doubtless surmised that its troubles had ended. But alas they had only just begun! Swallowing a prophet is one thing; digesting him is another. For three days and three nights the whale struggled desperately to digest Jonah, and for three days and nights Jonah obstinately refused to be digested. Never in the entire course of its life had it experienced such a difficulty. During the whole of that period, too, Jonah carried on a kind of prayer meeting, and the strange rumbling in its belly must have greatly added to the poor animal's discomfort At last it grew heartily sick of Jonah, and vomited him up on dry land. We have no doubt that it swam away into deep waters, a sadder but wiser whale; and that ever afterwards, instead of bolting its food, it narrowly scrutinised every morsel before swallowing it, to make sure it wasn't another prophet. According to its experience, prophets were decidedly the most unprofitable articles of consumption.

We are of course aware that the narrative states that "the Lord spake unto the fish, and it vomited Jonah upon the dry land." But this we conceive to be a mere pleasantry on the part of the unknown author. The idea of the Lord whispering into a whale's ear is ineffably ludicrous: besides, the whale had a very natural inclination to rid itself of Jonah, and needed no divine prompting.

Jonah's prayer "unto the Lord his God out of the fish's belly" is very amusing. There is not a sentence in it which bears any reference to the prophet's circumstances. It is a kind of Psalm, after the manner of those ascribed to David. Our belief is that the author found it floating about, and thinking it would do for Jonah, inserted it in his narrative, without even taking the trouble to furbish it into decent keeping with the situation.

The word of the Lord came unto Jonah a second time, and presuming no more to disobey, he went to Nineveh. It is to be supposed, however, that he first well-lined his poor stomach, for both he and the whale had fasted for three days and nights, and must have been sadly in want of victuals.

Nineveh, according to our author, was a stupendous city of "three days' journey." This means its diameter and not its circumference, for we are told that Jonah "entered into the city a day's journey." If we allow twenty miles as a moderate days' walk, Nineveh was sixty miles through from wall to wall, or about twenty times as large as London; and if densely populated like our metropolis, it must have contained more than eighty million inhabitants. This is too great a stretch even for a sailor's yarn. Our author did not take pains to clear his narrative of discrepancy. In his last verse he informs us that the city contained "more than six score thousand persons that cannot discern between their right hand and their left." If this number is correct Nineveh was a large place, but its dimensions were very much less than those stated in the Book of Jonah.

Jonah obeyed the Lord this time and began to preach. "Yet forty days," cried he, "and Nineveh shall be overthrown." How the prophet made himself understood is an open question! Either the Lord taught him their language, or he miraculously enabled them to understand Hebrew. Further, they worshipped Baal, and Jonah preached to them in the name of his foreign God. According to ancient, and to a large extent modern custom, we should expect them in such a case to kill the presumptuous prophet, or at least to shut him up as a madman. Yet they did nothing of the kind. On the contrary, "the people of Nineveh believed God." Even the king was converted. He covered himself with sackcloth, and sat in ashes. He also decreed that neither man nor beast in the city should eat or drink anything; but, said he, "let man and beast be covered with sackcloth, and cry mightily unto God: yea, let them turn every one from his evil way." What an enormous consumption of sackcloth there must have been! The merchants who sold it did a surprising business, and no doubt quotations went up immensely. We wonder, indeed, how they managed to supply such a sudden and universal demand. And what a sight was presented by the whole population of the city! Men, women, and children, high and low, rich and poor, were all arrayed in the same dingy garments. Even the horses, cows, pigs and sheep, were similarly attired. What a queer figure they must have cut! And what an astonishing chorus of prayer ascended to heaven! According to the text, the beasts had to "cry mightily" as well as the men. Since the confusion of tongues at Babel, neither history nor tradition records such a frightful hubbub.

Their supplications prevailed. God "saw their works, that they had turned from their evil way; and God repented of the evil, that he had said that he would do unto them; and he did it not." Immutable God changes his mind, infallible God repents!

God spared Nineveh, but only for a brief while, for it was destroyed a few years later by Arbaces, the Mede. The merciful respite was thus not of long continuance. Yet it "displeased Jonah exceedingly." He had been suspicious from the first, and he only fulfilled God's mission under constraint. And now his worst suspicions were confirmed. After he had told the Ninevites that their city would be overthrown in forty days, God had relented, and utterly ruined Jonah's reputation as a prophet. So he made himself a booth outside the city, and sat in its shadow, to watch what would happen, with a deep feeling, which he plainly expressed to the Almighty, that now his reputation was gone he might as well die. The Lord considerately "prepared a gourd," which grew up over Jonah's head to protect him from the heat; at which the sulky prophet was "exceedingly glad," although it would naturally be thought that the booth would afford ample protection. He, however, soon found himself sold; for the Lord prepared a worm to destroy the gourd, and when the sun arose he sent "a vehement east wind" which beat upon poor Jonah's head, and made him so faint that he once more asked God to despatch him out of his misery. Whereupon the Lord said coaxingly, "Doest thou well to be angry?" And Jonah pettishly answered, "Yes, I do." Then the Lord, with a wonderful access of pathos, altogether foreign to his general character, twitted Jonah with having pity for the gourd and none for the inhabitants of "that great city." With this the story concludes. We are unable to say whether the poor prophet, so wretchedly sold, ever recovered from his spleen, or whether it shortened his days and brought him to an untimely grave.

The Book of Jonah is as true as Gospel, for Jesus endorsed it. The Bible contains the truth, the whole truth, and nothing but the truth. So without expressing any sceptical sentiments, we will end by repeating Byron's words, "Truth is strange—stranger than fiction."

THE WANDERING JEWS

The Middle Ages had a legend of the Wandering Jew. This person was supposed to have been doomed, for the crime of mocking Jesus at the crucifixion, to wander over the earth until his second coming. No one believes this now. The true Wandering Jews were those slaves whom Jehovah rescued from Egyptian bondage, with a promise that he would lead them to a land flowing with milk and honey, but whom he compelled to roam the deserts instead for forty years, until all of them except two had perished. Of all the multitude who escaped from Egypt, only Joshua and Caleb entered the promised land. Even Moses had to die in sight of it.

These poor Wandering Jews demand our pity. They were guilty of many crimes against humanity, but they scarcely deserved such treatment as they received. Their God was worse than they. He was quick-tempered, unreasonable, cruel, revengeful, and dishonest. Few of his promises to them were performed. They worshipped a bankrupt deity. The land of promise was a Tantalus cup ever held to their lips, and ever mocking them when they essayed to drink. God was their greatest enemy instead of their best friend. Their tortuous path across the wilderness was marked by a track of bleaching bones. All the evils which imagination can conceive fell on their devoted heads. Bitten by serpents, visited by plagues, cursed with famine and drought, swallowed by earthquake, slain by war, and robbed by priests, they found Jehovah a harder despot than Pharaoh. Death was to them a happy release, and only the grave a shelter from the savagery of God.

Commentators explain that the Jews who left Egypt were unfit for the promised land. If so, they were unfit to be the chosen people of God. Why were they not allowed to remain in Egypt until they grew better, or why was not some other nation selected to inherit Canaan?

At the end of our number on "The Ten Plagues" we left the Jews on the safe side of the Red Sea. We must now ask a few questions which we had no space for then.

How, in a period of two hundred and fifteen years, did the seventy males of Jacob's house multiply into a nation of over two millions? Experience does not warrant belief in such a rapid increase. The Jewish chroniclers were fond of drawing the long bow. In the book of Judges, for instance, we are told that the Gileadites, under, Jephthah, slew 42,000 Ephriamites; and that the Benjamites slew 40,000 Israelites, after which the Israelites killed 43,000 Benjamites, all of these being "men of valor" that "drew the sword." The book of Samuel says that the Philistines had 30,000 war chariots, and that they slew 30,000 footmen of Israel. The second book of Chronicles says that Pekah, king of Israel, slew of Judah in one day 120,000 "sons of valor," and carried away 200,000 captives; that Abijah's force consisted of 400,000, and Jeroboam's of 800,000, 500,000 of whom were killed! At the battle of Waterloo the total number of men killed on our side was 4,172. The statistics of slaughter in the Bible were clearly developed from the inner consciousness of the Jewish scribes; and no doubt the same holds good with respect to the statistics of the flight from Egypt.

This view is corroborated by a singular statement in the third chapter of Numbers. We are there informed that when the census was taken "All the first-born males, from a month old and upwards of those that were numbered, were twenty and two thousand two hundred and three score and thirteen." Now as there were about 900,000 males altogether, it follows that every Jewish mother must have had on an average forty-two sons, to say nothing of daughters! Such extraordinary fecundity is unknown to the rest of the world, except in the reign of romance. The Jews bragged a great deal about Jehovah, and they appear to have obtained some compensation by bragging a great deal about themselves.

How did the Jews manage to quit Egypt in one night? There were 600,000 men on foot, besides women and children, not to mention "the mixed multitude that went up also with them." The entire population must have numbered more than two millions, and some commentators estimate it at nearly three. They had to come in from all parts of Goshen to Rameses, bringing with them the sick and infirm, the very old and the very young. Among such a large population there could not have been less than two hundred births a day. Many of the Jewish women, therefore, must have been just confined. How could they and their new-born children have started off in such a summary manner? Many more women must have been at the point of confinement How could these have been hurried off at all? Yet we are told that not a single person was left behind.

How were the flocks and herds driven out in such haste? There were about two million sheep and two hundred thousand oxen. The sheep alone would have required grazing-land as extensive as the whole county of Bedford, besides what would have been needed for the oxen. Is it credible that all these animals were collected together from such a wide area, and driven out of Egypt in one night? Yet we are told that not a single hoof was left behind!

How did the huge multitude of people march? If they travelled fifty men abreast, as is supposed to have been the practice in the Hebrew armies, the able-bodied warriors alone would have filled up the road for about seven miles, and the whole multitude would have formed a dense column twenty-two miles long. The front rank would have been two days' journey in advance of the rear.

How did the sheep and cattle march? How was it possible for them to keep pace with their human fellow-travellers? They would naturally not march in a compact array, and the vast drove must therefore have spread widely and lengthened out for miles.

What did the drove live upon during the journey from Barneses to Succoth, and from Succoth to Etham, and from Etham to the Red Sea? Such grass as there was, even if the sheep and cattle went before the men, women, and children, could not have been of much avail; for what was not eaten by the front ranks must have been trodden under foot at once, and rendered useless to those that followed. After they "encamped by the Red Sea," on the third day, there was no vegetation at all. The journey was over a desert, the surface of which was composed of hard gravel intermixed with pebbles. After crossing the Red Sea, their road lay over a desert region, covered with sand, gravel, and stone, for about nine miles; after which they entered a boundless desert plain, called El Ati white and painfully glaring to the eye; and beyond this the ground was broken by sand-hills. How were the two million sheep and two hundred thousand oxen provisioned during this journey?

What did the Jews themselves live on? The desert afforded them no sustenance until God miraculously sent manna. They must, therefore, have taken a month's provisions for every man, woman, and child. How could they possibly have provided themselves with so much food on so short a notice? And how could they have carried it, seeing that they were already burdened with kneading-troughs and other necessaries for domestic use, besides the treasures they "borrowed" of the Egyptians.

How did they provide themselves with tents? Allowing ten persons for each tent, they must have required two hundred thousand. Were these carefully got ready in expectation? In the land of Goshen they lived in houses with "lintels" and "side-posts." And how were the tents carried? The Jews themselves were already well loaded. Of course the oxen remain, but, as Colenso observes, they were not trained to carry t goods on their backs, and were sure to prove refractory under such a burden.

Whence did the Jews obtain their arms? According to Exodus (xiii, 18) "the children of Israel went up harnessed out of the land of Egypt." The Hebrew word which is rendered "harnessed" appears to mean "armed" or "in battle array" in all the other passages where it occurs, and is so translated. Some commentators, scenting a difficulty in this rendering, urge that the true meaning is "by five in a rank." But if 600,000 men marched out of Egypt "five in a rank," they must have formed a column sixty-eight miles long, and it would have taken several days to start them all off, whereas they went out altogether "that self-same day." Besides, the Jews had arms in the desert, and how could they have possessed them there unless they obtained them in Egypt? If they went out of Egypt "armed," why did they cry out "sore afraid" when Pharaoh pursued them?

According to Herodotus, the Egyptian army, which formed a distinct caste, never exceeded 160,000 men. Why were the Jews so appalled by less than a third of their own number? Must we suppose, with Kalisch, that their bondage in Egypt had crushed all valor and manhood out of their breasts? Josephus gives a different explanation. He says that the day after Pharaoh's host was drowned in the Red Sea, "Moses gathered together the weapons of the Egyptians, which were brought to the camp of the Hebrews by the current of the sea and the force of the wind assisting it. And he conjectured that this also happened by Divine Providence, that so they might not be destitute of weapons." But, as Colenso observes, though body-armor might have been obtained in this way, swords, spears and shields could not in any number. The Bible, too, says nothing about such an occurrence. We must therefore assume that 600,000 well-armed Jews were such utter cowards that they could not strike a blow for their wives and children and their own liberty against the smaller army of Pharaoh, but could only whimper and sigh after their old bondage. Yet a month later they fought bravely with the Amalekites, and ever afterwards they were as eager for battle as any Irishman at Donnybrook: fair. How can this difference be accounted for? Could a nation of hereditary cowards become stubborn warriors in the short space of a month?

Let us now follow the Wandering Jews through the Desert, which they should have crossed in a week or two, but which they travelled up and down for forty years. People who want to make an expeditious journey had better do without a divine guide.

Coming to Marah, they found only bitter water to drink, at which they began to murmur. But the Lord showed Moses a certain tree, which when cast into the water made it sweet. It must have been a wonderful tree to sweeten water for two millions of people. Bitter water, also, quenches thirst more readily than sweet, and it stimulates the appetite, which would be highly desirable under a fierce relaxing sun.

A month after they left Egypt they came to the wilderness of Sin. There they began to murmur again. Finding themselves without food, they remembered "the flesh pots" of Egypt, and reproached Moses with having brought them into the desert to die of hunger. Both Moses and the Lord seem to have thought it unreasonable on their part to ask for something to eat. Oliver Twist was stared at when he asked for more, but the Jews surprised God by asking for something to begin with. Yet reflecting, perhaps, that they were after all unable to live without food, the Lord rained down manna from heaven. After the dew evaporated in the morning, they found this heavenly diet lying on the ground. It was "like a coriander seed, white; and the taste of it was like wafers made with honey." No doubt the angels subsist on it in paradise. Moses preserved a pot of it for the instruction of future generations. The pot has, however, not been discovered up to the present day. Some future explorers may light upon it "in the fulness of time," and so-help to prove the historical character of the Pentateuch.

The manna, as might be expected, had some peculiarities. No matter how much or how little he gathered, every man found on measuring that he had exactly an omer of it. Although it fell regularly every week day, none fell on Sunday. A double quantity had, therefore, to be gathered on Saturday. It melted in the sun, but could nevertheless be baked and seethed. Any of it left overnight stank in the morning and bred worms.

For forty years "the children of Israel did eat manna." But more than once their gorge rose against it. Manna for breakfast, manna for lunch, manna for dinner, manna for tea, and manna for supper, was a little more than they could stand, The monotony of their diet became intolerable. Accordingly, we read in the twenty-first chapter of Numbers, that they complained of it and asked for a slight change in the bill of fare. "There is no bread," said they, "neither is there any water; and our soul loatheth this light food." This small request so incensed the Lord that he sent a lot of fiery serpents among them, which bit them so that "much people of Israel died." Like Oliver Twist, the Jews quickly repented their presumption. They humbled themselves before Moses, and he interceded with God for them. The prophet then made a brass serpent and set it on a pole, and on looking at it all who had been bitten recovered.

On another occasion, as we read in the eleventh of Numbers, they were guilty of a similar offence. This time it was the more surprising, as God had just burnt a lot of them up with raging fire for 'complaining.' They remembered "the fish, which we did eat in Egypt freely; the cucumbers, and the melons, and the leeks, and the onions, and the garlick." "Now," said they, "there is nothing at all, besides this manna, before our eyes-Who shall give us flesh to eat?" The Egyptian bill of fare was certainly enough to make their mouths water, and it proves that if Pharaoh made them work hard he did not starve them, as Jehovah very nearly succeeded in doing. They were so affected by their recollection of the luscious victuals they enjoyed in Egypt, that they actually cried with sorrow at their loss. Moses heard them weeping, "every man in the door of his tent." This put the Lord in a very bad temper; and Moses, who seems to have been much less irascible than Jehovah, "also was displeased." God determined to give them a surfeit. "Ye shall," said he, "not eat flesh one day, nor two days, nor five days, neither ten days nor twenty days; but even a whole month, until it come out at your nostrils, and be loathsome unto you." Thereupon the Lord sent a wind which brought quails from the sea. They were so plentiful that they fell in heaps two cubits high for about twenty miles around the camp. That worthy commentator, the Rev. Alexander Cruden, says that the miracle of this occurrence consisted, not in the great number of quails, but in their being "brought so seasonably" to the Jewish camp. The quantity did not trouble his credulous mind. "Some authors," says he, "affirm that in those eastern and southern countries, quails are innumerable, so that in one part of Italy within the compass of five miles, there were taken about an hundred thousand of them every day for a month together; and that sometimes they fly so thick over the sea, that being weary they fall into ships, sometimes in such numbers, that they sink them with their weight." The good man's easy reliance on 'some authors.' and his ready acceptance of such fables, show what credulity is engendered by belief in the Bible.

The Jews gathered quails for two days and a night, and joyfully carried them home. But "while the flesh was yet between their teeth," the Lord smote them with a very great plague, so that multitudes of them died. Poor devils! They were always in hot water.

How the sheep and cattle were provisioned the Bible does not inform us. There was scarcely a nibble of grass to be had in the desert, and as they could not very well have lived on sand and pebbles, they must have been supported miraculously. Perhaps the authors of the Pentateuch forgot all about this.

Not only were the Jews, like their flocks and herds, miraculously supported; they were also miraculously found in clothes. For forty years their garments and shoes did not wear out. How was this miracle wrought? When matter rubs against matter, particles are lost by abrasion. Did the Lord stop this process, or did he collect all the particles that were worn off during the day and replace them by night, on the soles of shoes, on the elbows of coats, and on the knees of pantaloons? If the clothes never wore out, it is fair to suppose that they remained absolutely unchanged. Imagine a toddling urchin, two years old at the exodus from Egypt, wearing the same rig when he grew up to manhood! Justin, however, says that the clothes grew with their growth. Some Jewish rabbis hold that angels acted as tailors in the wilderness, and so the garments were all kept straight. But Augustine, Chrysostom, and other Fathers abide by the literal interpretation that, through the blessing of God, the clothes and shoes never wore out, so that those who grew to manhood were able to hand them over, as good as new, to the rising generation. According to this theory, everybody must have had a poor fit, unless there was a transference of garments every twelve months or so.

The history of the Wandering Jews is full of miracles and wonders. It says that all the congregation of Israel, numbering over two millions, assembled at the door of the Tabernacle. As the whole width of the Tabernacle was eighteen feet, only nine men could have stood in front of it; and therefore the warriors of Israel alone, to say nothing of the rest of the population, if we allow eighteen inches between each rank of nine men, would have formed a column nearly twenty miles long! We find also that Moses, and Joshua after him, addressed not only the whole congregation of Israel, including men, women, and children, but the "mixed multitude" of strangers as well. Their voices were distinctly heard by a crowded mass of people as large as the entire population of London. They must have had stentorian lungs, or the people must have had a wonderful sense of hearing.

When the Jews were encamped, according to Scott's estimate, they lived in a sort of "moveable city, twelve miles square," nearly as large as London. The people had to go outside this vast camp every day to bring in a supply of water and fuel, after cutting the latter down where they could find it! All their rubbish had to be carried out in like manner, for Jehovah used sometimes to take a walk among them, and he was highly displeased at seeing dirt. Every man, woman, and child, including the old, the sick, and the infirm, had to go outside the camp to attend to the necessities of nature! All the refuse of their multitudinous sacrifices had to be lugged out of the camp by the three priests, Aaron, Eleazer, and Itharnar. Colenso reckons that the sacrifices alone, allowing less than three minutes for each, would have occupied them incessantly during the whole twenty-four hours of every day. The pigeons brought to them daily as sin offer-ings must have numbered about 264, and as these had to be consumed by the three priests, each of them had to eat 88 pigeons a day, besides heaps of roast beef and other victuals!

Soon after the first fall of manna, the Jews murmured again because they had no water. Whereupon Moses smote a rock with his magical rod, and water gushed from it. The precious fluid came just in time to refresh them for their fight with the Amalekites. These people were very obstinate foes, and it required a miracle to defeat them. Moses ascended a hill and held up his hand. While he did so the Israelites prevailed, but when he let down his hand the Amalekites prevailed. To ensure victory, Aaron and Hur stood on either side of him, and held up his hands until the sun set. By this means Joshua discomfited the Amalekites with great slaughter. Moses built an altar to celebrate the event, and God swore that he would "have war with Amelek from generation to generation." As Jehovah's vengeance was so lasting, it is no wonder that his worshipers carried on their wars ever afterwards on the most hellish principles.

In the thirty-first chapter of Numbers we read that 12,000 Israelites warred against Midian. The brag of the chronicler is evident in this number or in those which follow. This little army polished off all the kings of Midian, burnt all their cities and castles, slew 48,000 men, and carried off 100,000 captives, besides, 675,000 sheep, 72,000 oxen, and 61,000 asses. What prodigious spoil there was in those days! Of the captives Moses ordered 48,000 women and 20,000 boys to be massacred in cold blood; while the remaining 32,000 "women that had not known man by lying with him" were reserved for another fate. The Lord's share of these was thirty-two! They were of course handed over to the priests as his representatives. Parsons, who rail against the immorality of scepticism, say that this is all true.

These Midianites were a tough lot; for although they were all killed on this occasion, and their cities and castles burnt, we find them a powerful nation again in the sixth of Judges, and able to prevail against the Jews for seven years.

Another people badly punished by the Jews were the inhabitants of Bashan. All their cities were destroyed to the number of sixty. Their king, Og, was a gigantic fellow, and slept on an iron bed twelve feet long. The cities of Heshbon were destroyed in the same way. All the men, women, and children, were slaughtered. Not one was spared.

We shall hereafter follow the Jews under Joshua. For the present we must content ourselves with a last reference to their wanderings under Moses. While they were encamped round Mount Sinai, their leader received an invitation to go up and visit God who had been staying there for six days. They had much to talk about, and the interview lasted forty days and forty nights. At the end of it Moses descended, carrying with him the Ten Commandments, written by the finger of God on two tables of stone. In his absence the Wandering Jews had given him up as lost, and had induced Aaron to make them a god, in the shape of a golden calf, to go before them. This image they were worshipping as Moses approached the camp, and his anger waxed so not that he threw down the tables and broke all the Ten Commandments at once. He then burnt the calf in fire and ground it to powder, mixed it with water and made them drink it. He also sent the Levites among them, who put three thousand men to the edge of the sword. God wanted to destroy them altogether, but Moses held him back. "Let me alone," said the Lord. "No, no," said Moses, "just think what the Egyptians will say; they'll laugh at you after all as a poor sort of a god; and remember, too, that you are bound by an oath to multiply your people and to let them inherit the land of promise." So the Lord cooled down, and wrote out the Decalogue again on two fresh tables of stone. This Decalogue is supposed to be the foundation of morality. But long before the time of Moses moral laws were known and observed in Egypt, in India, and among all the peoples that ever lived. Moral laws are the permanent conditions of social health, and the fundamental ones must be observed wherever any form of society exists. Their ground and guarantee are to be found in human nature, and do not depend on a fabulous episode in the history of the Wandering Jews.

THE TOWER OF BABEL

The Bible, it is frequently asserted, was never meant to teach us science, but to instruct us in religion and morality; and therefore we must not look to it for a faithful account of what happened in the external world, but only for a record of the inner experiences of mankind. Astronomy will inform us how the heavenly bodies came into existence, and by what laws their motions are governed; Geology will acquaint us with the way in which the earth's crust was formed, and with the length of time occupied by the various stages of the process; and Biology will tell us all about the origin and development of living things. God has given us reason, by exercising which we may gather knowledge and establish sciences, so as to explain the past, illustrate the present, and predict the future; and as reason is sufficient for all this, there is no need of a divine revelation in such matters. But as reason is insufficient to teach the will of God and the laws of morality, a divine revelation of these is necessary, and the Bible contains it.

This plausible contention cannot, however, be maintained. The Bible is not silent with respect to astronomy, geology, or biology. It makes frequent and precise statements concerning them, and in nearly every instance it contradicts scientific truth as we have amply proved in previous numbers of this series.

The eleventh chapter of Genesis gives an explanation of the diversity of languages on the earth. It does this in the truest spirit of romance. Philologists like Max Müller and Whitney must regard the story of the Tower of Babel, and the confusion of tongues, as a capital joke. A great many parsons may still believe it, but they are not expected to know much.

One fact alone is enough to put the philology of Genesis out of court. The native languages of America are all closely related to each other, but they have no affinity with any language of the Old World. It is therefore clear that they could not have been imported into the New World by emigrants from the plains of Central Asia. The Genesaic theory is thus proved to be not of universal application, and consequently invalid.

Let us come to the Bible story. Some time after the Flood, and before the birth of Abraham, "the whole earth was of one language and one speech;" or, as Colenso translates the original, "of one lip, and of one language." This primitive tongue must have been Hebrew. God spoke it in Eden when he conversed with our first parents, and probably it is spoken in heaven to this day. For all we know it may be spoken in hell too. It probably is, for the Devil and his angels lived in heaven before they were turned into hell, and we may conclude that they took their native language with them. It was spoken by Adam when he named his wife in Paradise; by Eve, after the expulsion when she gave names to her sons, Cain and Seth; by Lamech, shortly before the Flood, when he explained the name of Noah; and indeed, as Colenso observes, "it is obvious that the names of the whole series of Patriarchs from Adam to Noah, and from Noah onwards, are in almost every instance pure Hebrew names." Delitzsch, however, thinks it comparatively more probable that the Syriac or Nabataan tongue, preserved after the dispersion at Babylon, was the one originally spoken. Yet he dismisses the possibility of demonstrating it. He supposes that the names of Adam and the other patriarchs have been altered, but not so as to lose any of their original meaning; in other words, that they have been, by God's grace, translated with perfect accuracy from the primeval speech. But Colenso very justly remarks that the original documents do not allude to a process of translation, and that we have no right to assume it. He also adds that "if the authority of Scripture is sufficient to prove the fact of a primeval language, it must also prove that this language was Hebrew."

Yet the Bible is wrong, for Hebrew could not have been the primitive speech. It is only a Semitic dialect, a branch of the Semitic stem. Sanscrit is another stem, equally ancient; and according to

Max Müller and Bunsen, both are modifications of an earlier and simpler language. Neither has the least affinity with Chinese, which again, like them, differs radically from the native dialects of America. As Hosea Biglow sings,

> "John P. Robinson, he
> Says they didn't know everything down in Judee."

And most certainly they did not know the true origin and development of the various languages spoken by the nations of the earth.

The people who dwelt on the earth after the Deluge, and all spoke one language, journeyed from the east, found a plain in, the land of Shinar, and dwelt there. Shinar is another name for Babylon. After dwelling there no one knows exactly how long, "they said one to another, Go to, let us make brick, and burn them throughly. And they had brick for stone, and slime had they for morter." The writer of this story was very fond of short cuts. It took men a long time to learn the art of making bricks; and the idea of their suddenly saying to each other "let us make brick," and at once proceeding to do so, is a wild absurdity.

Having made a lot of bricks, they naturally wished to do something with them. So "they said, Go to, let us build us a city and a tower, whose top may reach unto heaven; and let us make us a name, lest we be scattered abroad upon the face of the whole earth." How could making a name, for the information of nobody but themselves, prevent their dispersion? And how could they resolve to build a "city," when they had never seen one, and had no knowledge of what it was like? Cities are not built in this manner. "Rome wasn't built in a day" is a proverb which applies to all other places as well. London, Paris, and Rome, are the growth of centuries, and the same must have been true of ancient capitals.

The reason assigned by Scripture for the work of these primitive builders is plainly inadequate. A more probable reason is that they mistrusted God's promise never again to destroy the earth with a flood, and therefore determined to build a high tower, so that, if another deluge came, they might ascend above the waters, or, if need be step clean into heaven itself. Their lack of faith is not surprising. We find the same characteristic on the part of believers in our own day. They believe in God's promises only so far as it suits their interest and convenience. Scripture says, "Whoso giveth unto the poor lendeth unto the Lord." Yet there are thousands of rich Christians who seem to mistrust the security.

How high did these primitive builders think heaven was? According to Colenso, they said, "Come, let us build for us a city, and a tower with its head in heaven." Did they really think they would ever succeed in building so high? Perhaps they did, for their Natural Philosophy was extremely limited. They doubtless imagined the blue vault of heaven as a solid thing, in which were stuck the sun, moon, and stars, and no higher than the sailing clouds.

Their simple ignorance is intelligible, but how can we explain the ignorance of God? Their project alarmed him. He actually "came down to see the city and the tower which the children of men builded." Heaven was too distant for him to see from with accuracy, and telescopes were not then invented. A close inspection led him to believe that his ambitious children would succeed in their enterprise. They thought they might build into heaven, and he thought so too. What was to be done? If they once got into heaven, it might be very difficult to turn them out again. It took several days' hard fighting to expel Satan and the rebellious angels on a previous occasion, and these newcomers might be still more obstinate. In this dangerous extremity, "the Lord said [unto whom is unknown], Behold, the people is one, and they have all one language; and this they begin to do: and now nothing will be restrained from them which they have imagined to do. Go to, let us go down, and there confound their language, that they may not understand one another's speech."

Why did the Lord resolve to take all this trouble? Had he forgotten the law of gravitation and the principles of architecture? Was he, who made the heaven and the earth, ignorant of the distance between them? He had only to let the people go on building, and they would eventually confound themselves; for, after reaching a certain height, the tower would tumble about their ears. Gravitation would defeat the cohesion of morter Why did not God leave them alone? Why did he take so much unnecessary trouble? The answer is that this "Lord" was only "Jehovah" of the Jews, a tribal god, who naturally knew no more about the facts and laws of science than his worshippers who made him.

The Lord carried out his resolution. He "confounded their language," so that no man could understand his neighbors. Probably this judgment was executed in the night; and when they awoke in the morning, instead of using the old familiar tongue, one man spoke Chinese, another Sanscrit, another Coptic, another American, another Dutch, another Double Dutch, and so on to the end of the chapter.

According to the Bible, this is the true philology. No language on the earth is more than four thousand years old, and every one was miraculously originated at Babel. Is there a single philologist living who believes this? We do not know one.

The result of this confusion of tongues was that the people "left off to build the city," and were "scattered, abroad on the face of all the earth." But why did they disperse? Their common weakness should have kept them together. Society is founded upon our wants. Our necessity, and not our self-sufficiency, causes association and mutual helpfulness. Had these people kept company for a short time, they would have understood each other again. A few common words would have come into general use, and the building of the tower might have been resumed.

How was their language "confounded?" Did God destroy their verbal memory? Did he paralyse a part of their brain, so that, although they remembered the words, they could not speak them?

Did he affect the organs of articulation, so that the sounds of the primeval language could not be reproduced? Will some theologian kindly explain this mystery? Language is not a gift, but a growth. Different tribes and nations have had different experiences, different wants, and different surroundings, and the result is a difference in their languages, as well as in their religious ideas, political organisations, and social customs.

Before we leave this portion of the subject, we beg to introduce Milton again. In the last Book of "Paradise Lost" he adds from his fertile imagination to the Bible story, and supplies a few deficiencies about which the mind is naturally curious. He makes the Archangel Michael tell poor Adam and Eve, as part of his panoramic description of future times, that a mighty hunter shall arise, claiming dominion over his fellows, and gather under him a band of adherents. This is clearly Nimrod. Milton separates him and his subjects from the rest of mankind, and represents them as the people who settled on "the plain in the land of Shinar."

According to our great poet, therefore, the confusion of tongues applied only to them, and the other inhabitants of the earth retained the primeval language in all its original purity. This detachment, says Michael—

> *Marching from Eden towards the west, shall find*
> *The plain, wherein a black bituminous gurge,*
> *Boils out from underground, the mouth of Hell:*
> *Of brick, and of that stuff they cast to build*
> *A city and a tower, whose top may reach to Heaven;*
> *And get themselves a name, lest, far dispersed*
> *In foreign lands, their memory be lost,*
> *Regardless whether good or evil fame.*
> *But God, who oft descends to visit men*
> *Unseen, and through their habitations walks*
> *To mark their doings, them beholding soon,*
> *Comes down to see their city, ere the tower*
> *Obstruct Heav'n-tow'rs, and in derision sets*

> *Upon their tongue a various spirit to rase*
> *Quite out their native language, and instead*
> *To sow a jangling noise of words unknown.*
> *Forthwith a hideous gabble rises loud*
> *Among the builders; each to other calls*
> *Not understood, till hoarse, and all in rage,*
> *As mock'd, they storm: great laughter was in Heaven,*
> *And looking down, to see the hubbub strange*
> *And hear the din; thus was the building left*
> *Ridiculous, and the work Confusion named.*

If the Tower of Babel was built over the mouth of Hell it would be wise to explore its site and make proper excavations, so as to settle the geography and physical character of the bottomless-pit. The Churches are sadly in want of a little information about hell, and here is an opportunity for them to acquire it, We hope the explorers will all be selected for their extreme piety, so that they may be as fire-proof as Shadrach, Meshach, and Abednego, and happily escape cremation.

Because the Lord "did there confound their language" the place was "called Babel." The Hebrew root, balal to confound, is not, however, that from which the word "Babel" is derived, It is a compound of "Bel," and may mean the "House of Bel," "Court of Bel," or "Gate of Bel." Some, including Professor Rawlinson, suppose it be a compound of "El" or "il," in which case "Bab-El" means the "Gate of God."

It is evident that the story of the Tower of Babal was borrowed by the Jehovist author of this part of Genesis from the tradition of the famous unfinished Temple of Belus, one of the wonders of antiquity. "Birs Nimroud" is thus described by Kalisch:—

"The huge heap, in which bricks, stone, marble, and basalt, are irregularly mixed, covers a surface of 49,000 feet; while the chief mound is nearly 300 feet high, and from 200 to 400 feet in width, commanding an extensive view over a country of utter desolation.

The Tower consisted of seven distinct stages or square platforms, built of kiln-burnt bricks, each about twenty feet high, gradually diminishing in diameter. The upper part of the brickwork has a vitrefied appearance; for it is supposed that the Babylonians, in order to render their edifices more durable, submitted them to the heat of the furnace; and large fragments of such vitrefied and calcined materials are also intermixed with the rubbish at the base. This circumstance may have given rise to, or at least countenanced, the legend of the destruction of the Tower by heavenly fire, still extensively adopted among the Arabians. The terraces were devoted to the planets, and were differently colored in accordance with the notions of Sabæan astrology—the lowest, Saturn's, black; the second, Jupiter's, orange; the third, Mars, red; the fourth, the Sun's, yellow; the fifth, Venus's, white; the sixth, Mercury's, blue; the seventh, the Moon's, green. Merodach-adan-akhi is stated to have begun it B.C. 1100. It was finished five centuries afterwards by Nebuchadnezzar, who left a part of its history on two cylinders, which have lately been excavated on the spot, and thus deciphered by Rawlinson. 'The building, named the Planisphere, which was the wonder of Babylon, I have made and finished. With bricks, enriched with lapis lazuli, I have exalted its head. Behold now the building, named "The Stages of the Seven Spheres," which was the wonder of Borsippa, had been built by a former king. He had completed forty-two cubits of height: but he did not finish the head. From the lapse of time it became ruined. They had not taken care of the exit of the waters; so the rain and wet had penetrated into the brickwork. The casing of burnt brick lay scattered in heaps. Then Merodach, my great lord, inclined my heart to repair the building. I did not change its site, nor did I destroy its foundation-platform. But, in a fortunate month, and upon an auspicious day, I undertook the building of the raw-brick terrace and the burnt-brick casing of the Temple. I strengthened its foundation, and I placed a titular record on the part which I had rebuilt. I set my hand to build it up, and to exalt its summit. As it had been in ancient times, so I built up its structure. As it had been in former days, thus I exalted its head.'"

Professor Rawlinson assigns B.C. 2300 as the date of the building of the Temple. But as Colenso remarks, his reasoning is very loose. His date, however, is antecedent to the supposed time of the building of Babel, and according to his own chronology the latter may have been a tradition of the former. Add to this that the ruins of Birs Nimroud are extant, while there is no vestige of the ruins of Babel. According to Kalisch's chronology, Birs Nimroud was built long after the supposed time of Moses; and if he wrote the Pentateuch our position cannot be maintained. But he did not write the Pentateuch or any portion of it. The writer of the Jehovist portion of Genesis, which contains the story of the Tower of Babel, certainly did not flourish before the time of Solomon, about b.c. 1015—975. Here, then, is an interval of a century. That is a short period for the growth of a legend. Yet, as Colenso observes, "as the tower was apparently an observatory, and the fact of its being dedicated to the seven ancient planets shows that astronomical observations had made considerable progress among the Chaldeans at the time when it was built, the traditions connected with it may have embodied stories of a much earlier date, to which the new building gave fresh currency."

The Temple of Jupiter Belus with its tower was partially destroyed by Xerxes b.c. 490; upon which, says Kalisch, "the fraudulent priests appropriated to themselves the lands and enormous revenues attached to it, and seem, from this reason, to have been averse to its restoration." A part of the edifice still existed more than five centuries later, and was mentioned by Pliny. But the other part was, in the time of Alexander the Great, a vast heap of ruins. He determined to rebuild it, but desisted from the enterprise, when he found that ten thousand workmen could not remove the rubbish in two months. Benjamin of Tudela described it in the twelfth century, after which, for more than six hundred years, it remained unnoticed and unknown. The ruins were rediscovered by Niebuhr in 1756; subsequent explorers more accurately described them; and they were thoroughly examined, and their monumental records deciphered, about thirty years ago.

The myth attaching to it is not unique. As Kalisch observes, "most of the ancient nations possessed myths concerning impious giants, who attempted to storm heaven, either to share it with the immortal gods, or to expel them from it." And even the orthodox Delitzsch allows that "the Mexicans have a legend of a tower-building, as well as of a Flood. Xelhua, one of the seven giants rescued in the flood, built the great pyramid of Cholula, in order to reach heaven, until the gods, angry at his audacity, threw fire upon the building, and broke it down, whereupon every separate family received a language of its own." To lessen the force of this, Delitzsch says that the Mexican legend has been much colored by its narrators, chiefly Dominicans and Jesuits; but he is obliged to admit that there is great significance in the fact that the Mexican terrace-pyramid closely resembles the construction of the Temple of Belus. No argument can vitiate the conclusion that as similar myths to that of Genesis abounded in ancient times, it is highly illogical to attach particular importance to any one of them. If one is historic, all are historic. We are justified in holding that the Jewish story of the Tower of Babel is only a modification of the older story of the Temple of Belus.

We will conclude this Number by mentioning a few facts, not speculations, which are exceedingly curious, and which present grave difficulty to the orthodox believer.

According to the Bible, in Abraham's time, not four centuries after the Deluge, the descendants of Noah's three sons had multiplied into the four great kingdoms of Shinar (Babylon), Elam, Egypt, and Gerar, besides a multitude of smaller nations. Does any instructed man believe in the possibility of such multiplication? It is altogether incredible.

Some of these nations had reached a high degree of civilisation. Indeed, the temples, tombs, pyramids, manners, customs, and arts of Egypt betoken a full-grown nation. The sculptures of the Fourth Dynasty, the earliest extant, and which must be assigned to the date of about 3500 b.c., are almost as perfect as those of her Augustan age, two thousand years later. Professor Rawlinson seeks to obviate this difficulty by appealing to the version of the Seventy instead of to the Hebrew text, by which he obtains the remote antiquity of 8159 B.C., instead of 2848, for the Deluge. But this chronology does not reach within four hundred years of the civilisation denoted by the sculptures referred to! And there must have been milleniums of silent progress in Egypt before that period.

On the ancient monuments of Egypt the negro head, face, hair, form, and color, are the same as we observe in our own day. Consequently, the orthodox believer must hold that, in a few generations, the human family branched out into strongly marked varieties. History discountenances this assumption, and Biology plainly disproves it. Archdeacon Pratt supposes that Shem, Ham, and Japheth "had in them elements differing as widely as the Asiatic, the African, and the European, differ from each other." He forgets that they were brothers, sons of the same father and presumably of the same mother! Such extraordinary evolution throws Darwinism into the shade.

Noah lived fifty-eight years after the birth of Abraham. Shem lived a hundred and ten years after the birth of Isaac, and fifty years after the birth of Jacob. How was it that neither Abraham, Isaac, nor Jacob knew either of them. They were the most interesting and important men alive at the time. They had seen the world before the Flood. One of them had seen people who knew Adam. They had lived through the confusion of tongues at Babel, and were well acquainted with the whole history of the world. Yet they are never once mentioned in Scripture during all the centuries they survived their exit from the ark. Why is this? Noah before his death was the most venerable man existing. He was five hundred years older than any other man. He must have been an object of universal regard. Yet we have no record of the second half of his career; no account is given of his burial; no monument was erected to his memory. Who will explain this astounding neglect? The Bible is a strange book, and they are strange people who believe it.

BALAAM'S ASS

The ass has figured extensively in romance. His long ears and peculiar bray are explained by a story which goes back to the Flood. On that occasion, it is said, the male donkey was inadvertently left outside the ark, but being a good swimmer, he nevertheless managed to preserve his life. After many desperate efforts he at last succeeded in calling out the patriarch's name, as nearly as the vocal organs of a jackass would allow. "No-ah, No-ah," cried the forlorn beast. Noah's attention was at last aroused, and on looking out of window to see who was calling, he perceived the poor jackass almost spent and faintly battling with the waves. Quickly opening the window, he caught Neddy by the two ears and hauled him in. This he did with such vigor that Neddy's aural appendages were considerably elongated; and ever since donkeys have had long ears, and brayed "No-ah, No-ah" at the approach of wet weather. For the sake of Christians who are not well acquainted with God's Word, we add that this story is not in the Bible.

Classical scholars and students of modern literature know how the ass has been treated by poets and romancers. The stolid animal has generally been made the subject of comedy. Drunken and impotent Silenus, in the Pagan mythology, joins in the professions of Bacchus on a sober ass, and the patient animal staggers beneath the heavy burden of a fat-paunched tipsy god. Apulius and Lucian transform the hero of their common story into an ass, and in that shape he encounters the most surprising experiences. Voltaire makes an ass play a wonderful part in his "Pucelle." And in all these cases it is worth noticing how the profane wits remember the ass's relation to Priapian mysteries, from his fabled interruption of the garden-god's attempt on the nymph Lotis downwards, and assign to him marvellous amatory adventures. Erasmus, in his "Praise of Folly," does not forget the ass, with whom he compares the majority of men for stupidity, obstinacy, and lubricity; nor is the noble animal forgotten by Rabelais, who cracks many a joke and points many a witticism at his expense.

Our own genial humorist, Charles Lamb, confesses however to a deep tenderness for Neddy, and dwells with delight on the protection which his thick hide affords against the cruel usuage of man. He has, says Lamb, "a tegument impervious to ordinary stripes. The malice of a child or a weak hand can make feeble impressions on him. His back offers no mark to a puny foeman. To a common whip or switch his hide presents an absolute-insensibility. You might as well pretend to scourge a schoolboy with a tough pair of leather breeches on." Lamb also quotes the following passage from a tract printed in 1595, entitled "The Noblenesse of the Asse; a Work Rare, Learned, and Excellent": "He refuseth no burden; he goes whither he is sent, without any contradiction. He lifts not his foote against any one; he bytes not; he is no fugitive, nor malicious affected. He doth all-things in good sort, and to his liking that hath cause to employ him. If strokes be given him, he cares not for them." True, the ass is not much given to kicking or biting, but he has an awkward knack of quietly lying down when he is indisposed to work, and of rolling over with equal quietude if a rider happens to be on his back. But the old author is so enchanted with the "asse" that he does not stay to notice this scurvy trick. He even goes on to express his liking for the ass's bray, calling Neddy "a rare musitian," and saying that "to heare the musicke of five or six voices changed to so many of asses is amongst them to heare a song of world without end."

Sterne, in his "Sentimental Journey," has a chapter entitled "The Dead Ass," wherein the animal is lifted into the sphere of pathos. And lastly, Coleridge has some very pious musings on an ass, wherein the animal is lifted into the sphere of religion.

Now, dear reader, you begin to see the drift of this long exordium, although my purpose was indeed twofold. First, I wished, after the example of my betters in literature, to give you a slight glimpse of the immense extent of my learning. Secondly, I wished to lead you through the various stages of literary treatment of the ass, from the comic to the pathetic, and finally to the religious, in order that you might approach in a proper frame of mind the consideration of Balaam's ass, who is the most remarkable of all the four-legged asses mentioned in the Bible. There were others. Asses were being sought by Saul, the son of Kish, when he found a kingdom of subjects instead. Jesus rode into Jerusalem on an ass, and also apparently on a colt, having probably one leg over each. With the jawbone of an ass Samson slew a thousand Philistines; and if the rest of the animal accorded with that particular bone, he must have been a tough ass indeed. But all these are of little interest or importance beside the wonderful ass of the prophet Balaam, whose history is contained, with that of his master, in the twenty-second, twenty-third, and twenty-fourth chapters of the Book of Numbers.

Soon after the Wandering Jews in the desert were plagued by "fiery serpents" for asking Moses to give them a slight change in their monotonous bill of fare, they warred against the Amorites and pretty nearly exterminated them. Whereupon Balak the son of Zippor, king of Moab, grew "sore afraid." He called together the "elders of Midian" with those of Moab, and said that in his opinion the Jews would lick them all up as the ox licked up the grass of the field.

Against such a ferocious gang as the Jews, with a bloody God of Battles to help them, human valor promised little success; so Balak resolved to solicit supernatural aid. Accordingly he sent messengers unto Balaam the son of Beor, a renowned and potent soothsayer, desiring him to come and curse the people of Israel.

The King had implicit confidence in Balaam. "Whom thou blessest," said he, "is blessed, and whom thou cursest is cursed." This great prophet must have wrought prodigious wonders in his time to gain so magnificent a reputation; and if the king's panegyric on him was true, he must have been a dangerous person to those who annoyed him and made him swear.

The "elders of Moab and the elders of Midian," who were Balak's messengers, went to Pethor, where Balaam resided. As the reader might expect, they did not go empty-handed, but took with them "the rewards of divination." What these were we are not told. No doubt they were very handsome. The prophetical business requires large profits to compensate for the absence of quick returns; and in any case it is not to be supposed that a man who can do what no one else can, will begin work without a heavy retaining fee. We conclude that Balaam, like nearly every prophet mentioned in history, had a good eye for the main chance, and did not trust very much in the bounty of the gods. He was never hard up for bread and cheese while other people were hard up for divine assistance, and as that was an ignorant and credulous age, we presume that his larder was well-stocked. He must, indeed, have had a fine time, for he was the biggest pot in his own line of business in all that district.

Balaam knew his business well. It would never do for a prophet, a soothsayer, a wizard, or a diviner, to give prompt answers to his applicants, or even to make his answers plain when he does give them. That would render the profession cheap and rob it of mystery. So Balaam, therefore, said to the messengers, "Lodge here this night, and I will bring you word again, as the Lord shall speak unto me."

Now this reference to the Lord is very surprising. The Moabites worshipped Baal, and no doubt they had the utmost contempt for Jehovah. Yet Balaam, who was a prophet of their religion, tells them that he will consult the god of Israel on the subject of their visit! This is one of the self-contradictions with which the Bible abounds.

The next incident of the story is no less remarkable. God, the infinite spirit of the universe, paid Balaam a visit; and although he knows everything, past, present, and to come, he asked the prophet "What men are these with thee?" Balaam gave a straightforward reply, for he doubtless knew that prevarication and subterfuge were useless with God. Said he, "Balak the son of Zippor, King of Moab, has sent unto me, saying, Behold there is a people come out of Egypt, which covereth the face of the earth: come now, curse me them; peradventure I shall be able to overcome them and drive them out." The precision of Balaam's language is admirable, and so is its accuracy. He neither desired to keep the Lord in suspense, nor to leave him in ignorance of necessary details. God's answer was equally brief and perspicuous: "Thou shalt not go with them; thou shalt not curse the people: for they are blessed."

This interview between God and Balaam, like the following ones, occurred in the night. The Lord seems to have been always afraid of daylight, or else to have had a peculiar fondness for the dark. Perhaps he thought that during the night there was less chance of the conversation being interrupted, and it is well known that the Lord loves privacy and does not like conversing with more than one at a time. He agrees with us that "two's company and three's none."

In the morning Balaam got out of bed and told Balak's messengers to return and say that the Lord would not let him come; and they at once set out for the capital.

Balak, however, was not to be so easily put off. He seems to have regarded the prophet's talk about the Lord's prohibition as "all my eye." "Perhaps," said he to himself, "my messengers were small fry in the sight of Balaam, and he is therefore displeased. My presents also may have been too small I should have recollected that Balaam has a very exalted opinion of himself, and is renowned for his avarice. What a stupid I was, to-be sure. However, I'll try again. This time I'll send a deputation of big guns, and promise him great wealth and high position in the state. He can't refuse such a tempting offer." Straight-way he "sent yet again princes, more and more honorable" than those who went before, and commanded them to urge Balaam to let nothing hinder him from coming.

Balaam slightly resented this treatment. He told the messengers-that if Balak would give him his house full of silver and gold, he could not go beyond the word of the Lord, to do more or less. Yet he apparently deemed it politic to make another trial. He was, of course, quite aware that God is unchangeable, but somehow he thought the Lord might alter his mind. So he bade the messengers to tarry there that night while he consulted God afresh.

Balaam's expectation was realised. The Lord did change his mind. He "came unto Balaam at night, and said unto him, If the men come to call thee, rise up and go with them; but yet the word which I shall say unto thee, that shalt thou do." So the prophet rose up in the morning, saddled and mounted his wonderful ass, and went off with the princes of Moab.

Poor Balaam, however, did not reflect that as the Lord had changed his mind once he might change it twice, and the omission very nearly cost him his life. He was unfortunately ignorant of what happened to Moses on a similar occasion. After the Lord had dispatched the Jewish prophet to Egypt to rescue his people from bondage, he met him at an inn, where perhaps they both put up for the night, and sought to kill him. The same thing happened now. No sooner had Balaam set out on his journey than "God's anger was kindled against him because he went." This Jehovah is a queer God and dreadfully hard to please. If you don't obey his orders you run the risk of being damned, and if you do you stand a good chance of being murdered. The only safe course is to get out of his way and have nothing to do with him.

The "angel of the Lord" stood in Balaam's path, with a drawn sword in his hand, ready to kill the prophet whose only crime was having done exactly what he was told. But neither Balaam nor his two servants saw him. The ass, however, had better eyesight. Being only an ass, and not a man, he had a greater aptitude for seeing angels. Not liking the look of this formidable stranger, Neddy bolted from the pathway into a field. Balaam, who saw no reason for such behavior except sheer perverseness, began to whack his ass and tried to turn him[1] into the right road. Neddy succumbed to this

---

[1] Balaam's ass was a "she," but the sex is immaterial, and

forcible argument and jogged on again. The angel of the Lord had apparently, in the meantime, made himself invisible even to a jackass. His intention was ultimately to kill Balaam, but he delayed the fatal stroke in order to make the most of the comedy which he foresaw. Going a little in front, he "stood in a path of the vineyards, a wall being on this side, and a wall on that" Neddy caught sight of the angel again, and being unable this time to bolt into the field, he lurched against the wall, and gave Balaam's foot a good scrunching. Still the prophet suspected nothing out of the common, for that was an ordinary trick of refractory asses. Poor Neddy, therefore, got another thrashing. Then the angel of the Lord went on further, and "stood in a narrow place, where there was no way to turn either to the right hand or to the left." Neddy estimated the certain penalty of refusing to proceed and the probable penalty of going forward. After comparing them he decided to stop where he was, and then quietly laid down. Balaam's anger was once more kindled by this stupid obstinacy, and he whacked the ass again with his staff.

Then the Lord intervened, and brought about the most extraordinary incident of this wonderful story. He "opened the mouth of the ass," and lo! instead of braying Neddy spoke. Without a note of preparation he began to upbraid his master in good Moabitish. "What have I done," said he, "that thou hast smitten me these three times."

Singular to relate, Balaam was not in the least astonished at hearing an ass speak. He took it as quite an ordinary occurrence. One is almost inclined to think that the prophet and his donkey had held many a conversation before. In the Bible no one ever is astonished at anything, however wonderful. When the serpent accosted Eve in the garden of Eden, she was not at all surprised, but went on with the colloquy as though talking serpents were common things. If a dumb animal were nowadays to address a man with "How d'ye

---

as we commenced with the masculine gender we will continue with it.

do?" he would certainly be very much startled; but when the same thing occurred in the old Bible days, the man at once replied "Very well, thank you, how are you?"

Balaam promptly answered the ass's question. "Because," said he, "thou hast mocked me: I would there were a sword in mine hand, for now would I kill thee." Then the ass rejoined, "Am not I thine ass, upon which thou hast ridden ever since I was thine unto this day? Was I ever wont to do so unto thee?" This was a poser. Balaam scratched his head and reflected, but at last he was obliged to say "Nay."

Neddy had so far the best of the argument. But Balaam had the practical argument of the stick left, and no doubt he was about to convince the donkey with it. All arguments, practical or otherwise, would however have left the dispute exactly where it stood. Neddy saw the angel, and that was enough for him. Balaam did not see the angel, but only Neddy's obstinate stupidity. In short, they reasoned from different premises, and could not therefore arrive at the same conclusion. They might have argued till doomsday had not the Lord again intervened. He "opened Balaam's eyes," so that he also "saw the angel of the Lord standing in the way, and his sword drawn in his hand." Then Balaam "bowed his head, and fell flat on his face," and there he and Neddy laid side by side, two asses together.

Now, dear reader, you will observe that the ass, being indeed an ass, saw the angel first, and that Balaam, who was a wise man, did not see the angel until his wits were disordered by the wonder of a talking donkey. Does this not bear out great Bacon's remark that "in all superstition, wise men follow fools"? And may we not say, that if asses did not see angels first, wise men would never see them after?

The angel of the Lord said to Balaam, while he remained flat on his face, "Wherefore hast thou smitten thine ass these three times? behold, I went out to withstand thee, because thy way is perverse before me: and the ass saw me, and turned from me these three times: unless she had turned from me, surely now also I had slain thee, and saved her alive." The moral of this is that asses stand the best chance of salvation, and that wise men run a frightful risk of damnation until they lose their wits.

Balaam recognised the awful mess he was in, and being by this time as limp as a wet rag, he made the most abject apology. "I have sinned," he said, "for I knew not that thou stoodest in the way against me." This strange reasoning shows still more clearly how the poor prophet had taken leave of his senses. He had not sinned at all, for he was strictly obeying God's commands; nor was it his fault that the angel remained so long invisible. When the Lord "opened his eyes," and made his vision like unto the vision of an ass, he saw the angel plainly enough; and how could he possibly have done so before?

"I'll go back," added Balaam, thinking that if he sinned so greatly in going forward, he had better return home. But the angel of the Lord, who had intended to kill him for advancing, now told him to "go with the men." And Balaam went with them, keeping his weather eye open during the rest of the journey.

Balak was heartily glad to see Balaam. The prophet had been a long time coming, but better late than never. The next day they went "up into the high places of Baal," from which they could see the utmost part of the people of Israel. "There they are," said Balak, "confound them! leprous slaves out of Egypt, bent on stealing other people's lands, and sticking to all they can lay hands on; bloodthirsty vagabonds, who fight people with whom they have no quarrel, and kill men, women, and children when they are victorious. Now, Balaam, do your duty. Curse them, and lay it on thick."

Seven altars were built, and seven oxen and seven rams sacrificed on them. But all this good meat was wasted, for when Balaam "went to an high place," God met him, according to agreement, and told him what to say. And lo! when the prophet returned to the king, he blessed the Jews instead of cursing them.

"Hullo, Balaam, what's this?" cried the king. "I asked you to curse my enemies and you've gone and blessed them. What d'ye mean?" "True," answered Balaam, "but I told you that I could only speak what the Lord put into my mouth."

Balak appears to have been just as sceptical as Pharaoh about the God of the Jews. He attributed his disappointment to a freak of the prophet, and not being easily baffled he resolved to try again. So he took Balaam up another high place, and built seven fresh altars, and sacrificed on them seven more bullocks and rams; after which he repeated his invitation. Again Balaam went farther to consult the Lord, whom he found waiting for him, and received his instructions. And lo! when he returned to Balak he again blessed the Jews instead of cursing them.

Balak resolved to try again. He took Balaam to another high place, built seven more altars, and sacrificed seven more bullocks and seven more rams. But again the prophet blessed Israel, and a third time the king was sold. Then he gave it up, and Balaam and his ass went home.

What became of the ass is unknown. Perhaps he went into the prophetical business himself, and eventually retired on a very handsome fortune. Perhaps he went about as a preacher of the gospel as it was then understood; in which case, judging from the rule of success in later ages, we have no doubt that he attracted large audiences and delighted all who were fortunate enough to sit under him. And when he died all the two-legged asses in Moab probably wept and refused to be comforted.

Balaam's end was tragic. The thirteenth chapter of Joshua informs us that he was eventually slain by the very people he had thrice blessed. After an account of one of the bloody wars of Jehovah's bandits we read that "Balaam also the son of Beor, the sooth-sayer, did the children of Israel slay with the sword among them that were slain by them." The angel of the Lord spared him, but God's butchers cut his throat at last. On the whole he might as well have cursed the Jews up and down to Balak's satisfaction, and taken the handsome rewards which were offered him on such easy terms.

Here endeth the story of Balaam's Ass. I hope my reader still believes it, for if not, he will be reprobate while he lives and damned when he dies.

GOD'S THIEVES IN CANAAN

Some years ago the righteous indignation of England was roused by the daily record of atrocities perpetrated in Bulgaria by the Turkish bashi-bazouks. Men were wantonly massacred, pregnant women ripped up, and maidens outraged by brutal lust. Our greatest statesman uttered a clarion-cry which pealed through the whole nation, and the friends of the Turk in high places shrank abashed and dismayed before the stern response of the people. Many clergymen attended public meetings, and denounced not only the Turks, but also their Mohammedanism. They alleged that the Koran sanctioned, even if it did not command, the horrors which had been wrought in Eastern Europe, and they declared that there was no hope for a country which derived its maxims of state from such an accursed book. Those denunciations did honor to their hearts, but very little to their heads. For every brutal injunction in the Koran, twenty might be found in the Bible. Before the clergy cry out against the Scriptures of Islam, they should purge their own of those horrid features which are an insult to man and a blasphemy against God. Mohammed gave savage counsels to his followers with respect to waging war, but these sink into insignificance beside the counsels given to the Jews by Moses in the name of God.

Bible Romances are generally comic, but this one is infinitely tragic. The whole range of history affords no worse instances of cold-blooded cruelty than those which God's thieves, the Jews, perpetrated in Canaan, when they took forcible possession of cities they had not built and fields they had never ploughed. "How that red rain will make the harvest grow!" exclaims Byron of the blood shed at Waterloo; and surely the first harvests reaped by the Jews in Canaan must have been luxuriantly rich, for the ground had been drenched with the blood of the slain.

Before Moses died, according to the Bible, he delivered an elaborate code of laws to his people in the name of God. The portions referring to war are contained in the twentieth chapter of Deuteronomy. Here they stand in all their naked hideous-ness:—

"When thou comest nigh unto a city to fight against it, then proclaim peace unto it. And it shall be, if it make thee answer of peace, and open unto thee, then it shall be that all the people that is found therein shall be tributaries unto thee, and they shall serve thee. And if it will make no peace with thee, but will make war against thee, then thou shalt besiege it. And when the Lord thy God hath delivered it into thine hands, thou shalt smite every male thereof with the edge of the sword: But the women, and the little ones, and the cattle, and all that is in the city, even all the spoil thereof, shalt thou take unto thyself; and thou shalt eat the spoil of thine enemies, which the Lord thy God hath given thee. Thus shalt thou do unto all the cities which are very far off from thee, which are not of the cities of these nations. But of the cities of these people, which the Lord thy God doth give thee for an inheritance, thou shalt save alive nothing that breatheth. But thou shalt utterly destroy them."

Such were the fiendish commands of Jehovah, the bloody maxims of inspired war. Let us see how the Jews carried them out.

During the lifetime of Moses they made a good beginning; for in their war against Midian they slew 48,000 men, 48,000 women, and 20,000 boys, and took as spoil 32,000 virgins. But they did much better under Joshua.

After God had dispatched Moses and secretly buried him, so that nobody should ever discover his sepulchre, Joshua was appointed leader in his stead. He was "full of the spirit of wisdom, for Moses had laid his hands upon him." Then, as now, religious superiors transmitted holiness to their inferiors through the skull. God accepted the nomination of Moses and instructed Joshua in his duties. He told him to be above all "strong and very courageous," and to fight the enemy according to the law of Moses. Joshua was not the man to neglect such advice.

Joshua was soon ordered to cross the river Jordan and begin the holy war. But before doing so, he dispatched two spies to reconnoitre Jericho, the first place to be attacked. They reached the city by night, and of course required lodgings. Instinct led them to the house of Rahab, the harlot. She proved a very good friend; for when messengers came from the king in the morning to inquire about them, she said that they had gone, and advised the messengers to go after them, which they did. Meanwhile she hid the spies under some flax on the roof of her house, and at night "let them down by a cord through the window, for she dwelt on the town wall." Before they left, however, she made a covenant with them. Like many other ladies of easy virtue, or no virtue at all, Rahab was piously inclined. She had conceived a great respect for Jehovah, and was assured that his people would overcome all their enemies. But she had also a great respect for her own skin; so she made the two spies promise on behalf of the Jews that when they took Jericho they would spare her and all her relatives; and they were to recognise her house by the "line of scarlet thread in the window." They got back safe to Joshua and told him it was all right; the people were in a dreadful funk, and all the land would soon be theirs.

Joshua got up early the next morning and told the Jews that the Lord was going to do wonders. They wanted to get "on the other side of Jordan," and the Lord meant to ferry them across in his own style. Twelve men were selected, one from each tribe, to follow the priests who bore the ark in front, and all the Jewish host came after them. As it was harvest time, the river had overflowed its banks. When the priests' feet "were dipped in the brim of the water," the river parted in twain; on one side the waters "stood and rose up upon an heap," while on the other side they "failed and were cut off." As no miracle was worked further up the river to stop the supplies, the "heap" must have been a pretty big one before the play ended. A clear passage having been made, the Jews all crossed on dry ground. They seem to have done this in less than a day, but three millions of people could not march past one spot in less than a week. Perhaps the Lord gave them a shove behind.

The twelve selected Jews, one from each tribe, took twelve big stones out of the bed of the river, which were "pitched in Gilgal" as "a memorial unto the children of Israel for ever." For ever is a long time and is not yet ended. Those stones should be there now. Why don't the clergy try to discover them? If brought to London and set up on the Thames embankment they would throw Cleopatra's needle into the shade.

When God had ferried the Jews across, and picked out the twelve big stones as aids to memory, the "heap" of water tumbled down and overflowed the banks of the river. Joshua and his people then encamped near Jericho, in readiness for greater wonders to come.

Three days afterwards the manna ceased. Jehovah's fighting cocks wanted a more invigorating diet. This time they did not ask for a change, but the Lord vouchsafed it spontaneously.

All the males, too, were circumcised by God's orders. This Jewish rite had been neglected during the forty years' wandering in the wilderness, but it was now resumed. From the text it seems that Joshua circumcised all the males himself. As they numbered about a million and a half it must have been a long job. Allowing a minute for each amputation, it would in the natural course of things have taken him about three years to do them all; but being divinely aided, he finished his task in a single day. Samson's jaw-bone was nothing to Joshua's knife.

Soon after Joshua, being near Jericho, like Balaam's ass saw an angel with a drawn sword in his hand. When he had made obeisance, by falling flat and taking off his shoes, he received from this heavenly messenger precise instructions as to the capture of the doomed city. The Lord's way of storming fortresses is unique in military literature. Said he to Joshua—"Ye shall compass the city, all ye men of war, and go round about the city once. Thus shalt thou do six days. And seven priests shall bear before the ark seven trumpets of rams' horns: and the seventh day ye shall compass the city seven times, and the priests shall blow with the trumpet? And it shall come to pass that when they make a long blast with the ram's horn, and when ye hear the sound of the trumpet all the people shall shout with a great shout; and the wall of the city shall fall down flat, and the people shall ascend up every man straight before him."

Did ever another general receive such extraordinary instructions from his commander-in-chief? God's soldiers need no cannon, or battering rams, or bombshells; all they require is a few rams' horns and good lungs for shouting.

God's orders were obeyed. Six days in succession did the Jews march round the walls of Jericho, no doubt to the great bewilderment of its inhabitants, who probably wondered why they didn't come on, and felt that there was something uncanny in this roundabout siege. On the seventh day they went round the city seven times. How tired they must have been! Jericho, being a capital city, could not have been less than several miles in circumference. The priests blew with the trumpets, the people shouted with a great shout, and the walls of Jericho fell flat—as flat as the simpletons who believe it.

A scene of horror ensued. The Jews "utterly destroyed all there was in the city, both man and woman, young and old, and ox, and sheep, and ass, with the edge of the sword." Only Rahab and her relatives were spared. The silver, and the gold, and the vessels of brass and of iron, were put into the Lord's treasury—that is, handed over to the priests; and then the city was burnt with fire. God commanded this, and his chosen people executed it Could Jericho have been treated worse if the Devil himself had planned the fight, and the vilest fiends from hell had conducted it?

Rahab the harlot, being saved with all her relatives, who were perhaps as bad as she, dwelt with the Jews ever afterwards. Whether she continued in her old profession we are unable to say.

But it is certain that the Jews soon after grew very corrupt, and the Lord's anger was kindled against them. The first result of God's displeasure was that the Jews became demoralised as warriors. Three thousand of them, who went up against Ai, were routed, and thirty-six of them were slain. This seems a very small number, but, as we have already observed, the Jewish chroniclers were much given to bragging. Their losses were always very small, and the enemy's very great.

After this rebuff the Jews funked; their hearts "melted and became as water." Joshua rent his clothes, fell upon his face before the ark, and remained there until the evening. The elders of Israel did likewise, and they all put dust on their heads. To conclude the performance Joshua expostulated with God, asked him whether he had brought his people over Jordan only to betray them to their enemies, and expressed a hearty wish that they had never crossed the river at all.

The Lord told Joshua to get up, as it was no use lying there. Israel had sinned, and God had determined not to help them until they had purged themselves. Some one, in fact, had stolen a portion of the spoil of Jericho, all of which belonged to the Lord, that is to the priests, who evidently helped to concoct this pretty story. Joshua forthwith proceeded to hunt the sinner out. His method was very singular. He resolved to go through the twelve tribes until the culprit was found. The tribe of Judah was examined first, and luckily in the very first family "Achan was taken," although we are not told how he was spotted. Achan confessed that he had appropriated of the spoil a "goodly Babylonish garment, and two hundred shekels of silver, and a wedge of gold of fifty shekels weight," which he had hidden under his tent. His doom was swift and terrible; he was stoned to death, and his body burnt with fire. We may think his punishment severe, but we cannot deny his guilt. He, however, was not the only sufferer. Jehovah was not to be satisfied with a small quantity of blood. Achans's sons and daughters were stoned with him, and their bodies were burnt like his. His very oxen, asses, and sheep were served in the same manner. A great heap of stones was raised over their cinders, and then "the Lord turned from the fierceness of his anger." Jehovah acted just like the savage old chieftain of a savage tribe. As irascible tempers do not improve with age, we presume that he is still as peppery as ever. Yet we are asked to love, venerate, and worship this brutal being, as the ideal of all that is merciful, just, and pure.

Immediately after Joshua sent thirty thousand men against Ai, which they took with great ease. All its inhabitants, from the oldest man to the youngest babe, were massacred. The city itself was burnt into a desolate heap. The King of Ai was reserved to furnish the Jews with a little extra sport, by way of dessert to the bloody feast. He was hanged on a tree until eventide, when his carcass was taken down and "buried under a heap of stones." Joshua "then built an altar unto the Lord God of Israel in mount Ebal," who appears to have been mightily well pleased with the whole business.

Joshua's next exploit was indeed miraculous. He gathered all the Jews together, men, women, children, and even the strangers, and read to them all the laws of Moses, without omitting a single word. It must have been a long job, and Joshua's throat must have been rather dry at the end. But the greatest wonder is how he made himself heard to three millions of people at once. No other orator ever addressed so big an audience. Either their ears were very sharp, or his voice was terribly loud. The people in the front rank must have been nearly stunned with the sound. Joshua could outroar Bottom the weaver by two or three miles.

The people of Gibeon, by means of messengers who palmed themselves off on Joshua as strangers from a distant country, contrived to obtain a league whereby their lives were spared. When their craft was detected they were sentenced to become hewers of wood and drawers of water to the Jews; in other words, their slaves.

Adoni-zedec, king of Jerusalem; Hoham, king of Hebron; Piram, king of Jamuth; Japhia, king of Lachish; and Debir, king of Eglon;

banded themselves together to punish Gibeon for making peace with the Jews. Joshua went with all his army to their relief. He fell upon the armies of the five kings, discomfitted them with great slaughter, and chased them along the way to Beth-horon. As they fled the Lord joined in the hunt. He "cast down great stones from heaven upon them" and killed a huge number, even "more than they whom the children of Israel slew with the sword."

When we read that Pan fought with the Greeks against the Persians at Marathon, we must regard it as a fable; but when we read that Jehovah fought with the Jews against the five kings at Gibeon, we must regard it as historical truth, and if we doubt it we shall be eternally damned.

Not only did the Lord join in the war-hunt, but Joshua wrought the greatest miracle on record by causing a stationary body to stand still. He stopped the sun from "going down" and lengthened out the day for about twelve hours, in order that the Jews might see to pursue and kill the flying foe. "The sun stood still, and the moon stayed, until the people had avenged themselves upon their enemies." What Joshua really stopped, if he stopped anything, was the earth, for its revolution, and not the motion of the sun, causes the phenomena of day and night. Science tells us that the arrest of the earth's motion would generate a frightful quantity of heat, enough to cause a general conflagration. Yet nothing of the kind happened. How is it, too, that no other ancient people has preserved any record of this marvellous occurrence? The Egyptians, for instance, carefully noted eclipses and such events, but they jotted down no memorandum of Joshua's supreme miracle. Why is this? How can Christians explain it?

When Jupiter personated Amphytrion, and visited his bride Alcmena, the amorous god lengthened out the night in order to prolong his enjoyment. Why may we not believe this? Is it not as credible, and quite as moral, as the Bible story of Jehovah's lengthening out the day to prolong a massacre? Were the Greeks any bigger liars than the Jews?

It has been suggested that Joshua was so elated with the victory that he drank more than was good for him, and got in such a state that in the evening he saw two moons instead of one. Nobody liked to contradict him, but the elders of Israel, to harmonise their leader's vision, declared that it comprised the sun and the moon, instead of two moons, which were clearly absurd. The court poet improved on this explanation, and composed the neat little poem which is partially preserved by the Jewish chronicler, who asks "Is not this written in the book of Jasher?" The waggish laureate Jasher is supposed by some profane speculators to have got up the whole miracle himself.

The five kings fled with their armies and "hid themselves in a cave at Makkedah." Joshua ordered the mouth to be closed with big stones until the pursuit was ended. At last they were brought out and treated with great ignominy. Their necks were made footstools of by the captains of Israel, and they were afterwards hung on trees until the evening, when their carcasses were flung into the cave. After this highly civilised treatment of their captives, the Jews took all the capital cities of these five kings and slew all the inhabitants. Then they desolated the hills and vales. Joshua "left none remaining, but utterly destroyed all that breathed, as the Lord God of Israel commanded." Hazor and many other places were also treated in the same way, "there was not any left to breathe."

Jehovah was not, however, able to execute his intentions completely. The children of Judah could not drive the Jebusites out of Jerusalem; nor could the children of Manasseh entirely drive out the Canaanites from their cities. After Joshua's death, as we read in the book of Judges, "the Lord was with Judah, and he drave out the inhabitants of the mountain; but could not drive out the inhabitants of the valley, because they had chariots of iron." Iron chariots were too strong for the Almighty! Yet he managed to take off the wheels of Pharaoh's chariots at the Red Sea. Why could he not do the same on this occasion? Were the linch-pins too tight or the wheels too heavy?

Joshua died at the ripe old age of a hundred and ten. Whatever else he may have been, he was certainly one of the gamest fighting cocks that ever lived. Jehovah never found a better instrument for his bloody purposes. They buried him at Timnath-serah. Joseph's old bones, which Moses brought out of Egypt, were buried at Shechem. Had they been kept much longer some Hebrew "old-clo' man" might have carried them off and made an honest penny by them.

After Joshua's death, the tribe of Judah fought against Adoni-bezek. When they caught him they cut off his thumbs and his big toes. He acknowledged the justice of his punishment, and admitted that God had served him just as he had himself served seventy kings, whose great toes he had cut off, and made them eat under his table. Kings must have been very plentiful in those days.

During Joshua's lifetime the Jews served God, and they kept pretty straight during the lifetime of the elders who had known him. But directly these died they went astray; "they forsook the Lord and worshipped Baal and Ashtaroth." God punished them by letting their enemies oppress them. "Nevertheless," says the story, "the Lord raised up judges, which delivered them out of the hand of those that spoiled them. And yet they would not hearken unto their judges, but they went a whoring after other gods, and bowed themselves unto them; and they turned quickly out of the way which their fathers walked in, obeying the commandments of the Lord; but they did not so..... And it came to pass, when the judge was dead, that they returned and corrupted themselves more than their fathers, in following other Gods to serve them, and to bow down unto them; they ceased not from their own doings, nor from their stubborn way."

God's selection of the Jews as his favorite people does not seem to reflect much credit on his sagacity. All who came out of Egypt, except two persons, turned out so badly that they were pronounced unfit to enter the promised land, and doomed to die in the wilderness. The new generation who entered Canaan, after being circumcised to make them holy; after seeing the miracles of Jordan and the valley of Ajalon; after having gained a home by God's assistance in a land flowing with milk and honey; this very generation proved worse than their fathers. The original inhabitants of Canaan, whom they dispossessed, could hardly have surpassed them in sin against Jehovah; and therefore the ruthless slaughter of their conquest was as unreasonable as it was inhuman. So much for "God's Thieves in Canaan."

CAIN AND ABEL

God completed the immense labors described in the first chapter of Genesis by creating man "in his own image," after which he serenely contemplated "everything that he had made, and; behold, it was very good." Yet the first woman deceived her husband, the first man was duped, and their first son was a murderer. God could not have looked very far ahead when he pronounced everything "very good." It is clear that the original pair of human beings were very badly made. As the Lord was obliged to take a rest on the seventh day, it is not unreasonable to suppose that he was pretty tired on the sixth, and scamped the work. All the sin and suffering in this world is the consequence of man having been the fag-end of creation. If the Lord had rested on the sixth day and created man on the seventh, how different things might have been! The Devil would probably have done no business in this world, and the population of hell would be no more now than it was six thousand years ago.

After leaving the Garden of Eden, Adam and Eve, having no fear of Malthus in their hearts, began to "multiply and replenish the earth." When their first child was born, Eve said, "I have gotten a man from the Lord," poor Adam's share in the youngster's advent being quietly ignored. She christened him Cain, a name which comes from a Hebrew root signifying to acquire. Cain was regarded as an acquisition, and his mother was very proud of him. The time came when she wished he had never been born.

Some time after, but how long is unknown, Eve gave birth to a second son, called Abel. Josephus explains this name as meaning grief, but Hebrew scholars at present explain it as meaning nothingness, vanity, frailty. The etymology of Abel's name shows conclusively that the story is a myth. Why should Eve give her second boy so sinister a name? How could she have so clearly anticipated his sad fate? Cain's name has, too, another significance besides that of "acquisition," for, as Kalisch points out, it also belongs to the Hebrew verb to strike, and "signifies either the man of violence and the sire of murderers, or the ancestor of the inventors of iron instruments and of weapons of destruction."

Cain and Abel had to get their own living. Being born after the Fall, they were of course debarred from the felicities of Eden, and were compelled to earn their bread by the sweat of their brows, in accordance with God's wide-reaching curse. Both, so to speak, were forced to deal in provisions. Abel went in for meat, and Cain for vegetables. This was an admirable division of labor, and they ought to have got on very well together; one finding beef and mutton for dinner, and the other potatoes and greens. They might even have paid each other handsome compliments across the table. Abel might have said "My dear Cain, these vegetables are first-rate," and Cain might have replied, "My dear Abel, I never tasted a better cut."

Delitzsch, whose criticisms are huge jokes, frowns on this picture of fraternal peace. He opines that Cain and Abel were vegetarians and never enjoyed a beef-steak or a mutton-chop. Abel kept only small domestic cattle, such as sheep and goats, whose woolly skin might be used to cover "their sinful nakedness." The utmost Delitzsch allows is that they perhaps drank milk, which, although animal nutriment, is not obtained through the destruction of animal life. But, as Colenso observes, animals were slain for sacrifices, and they may have been killed also for eating. Besides, even a vegetable diet involves infinite destruction of minute animal life. On the whole we prefer to disregard Delitzsch in this matter, and to stand by our pleasant picture of the two first brothers at dinner.

Their admirable arrangement, however, brought mischief in the end. It was right enough so far as they were concerned, but it worked badly in relation to God. They liked a mixed diet, but the Lord was purely carnivorous and liked all meat. He devoured Abel's provisions with great relish, but turned up his nose at Cain's vegetables. The mealiest potatoes, the tenderest green peas, had no charm for him; and even the leeks, the garlic, the onions, and the cucumbers, which were afterwards so beloved by his Jewish favorites, were quite unattractive. In the language of Scripture, "Cain brought of the fruit of the ground an offering unto the Lord. And Abel, he also brought of the firstlings of his flock and of the fat thereof. And the Lord had respect unto Abel and to his offering: But unto Cain and to his offering he had no respect" Elsewhere in the Bible we read "God is no respecter of persons," but Scripture is full of contradictions, and such things present no difficulty to the spirit of faith, which, like hope, "believeth all things."

Why was Cain's offering slighted? The Bible does not tell us, but many reasons have been advanced by commentators. The Talmud supposes that Cain did not offer his best produce, but only the inferior kinds, thus giving God what he did not require himself, and treating the holy rite of sacrifice as a means of working off his refuse vegetables. Kalisch waives this theory, and thinks it probable that Cain's sin was primarily not against God, but against man. "The supposition," he says, "is obvious that envy and jealousy had long filled the heart of Cain, when he contrasted his laborious and toilsome life with the pleasant and easy existence of his brother Abel. With incessant exertion, tormented by anxiety, and helplessly dependent on the uncertainty of the skies, he forced a scanty subsistence out of the womb of the repugnant soil; whilst his brother enjoyed a life of security and abundance, in the midst of rich valleys, beautiful hills, and charming rural scenes. And while he envied Abel's prosperity, he despised his idleness, which was indebted for the necessaries of life to the liberality of nature, rather than to personal exertions. This hatred and jealousy took root in Cain's heart. He beheld the happiness of his brother with the feelings-of an enemy. The joy at the success of his own labors was embittered by the aspect of his brother's greater affluence. How could God look with delight upon an offering which the offerer himself did not regard with unalloyed satisfaction? How could he encourage by his applause a man whose heart was poisoned by the mean and miserable passion of envy?"

But all this is gratuitous and far-fetched. Cain was not afflicted with so laborious an occupation. Adam supported himself and Eve, and all Cain had to do was to provide himself, and perhaps Abel, with vegetables. Nor could Abel's occupation have been light, for flocks and herds require a good deal of attendance, and in those early days they needed vigilant protection against the ravages of wild beasts. Abel's task must have been quite as heavy as Cain's. Our opinion is that the Lord showed his usual caprice, hating whom he would and loving whom he would. Jehovah acted like the savage hero of Mr. Browning's "Caliban on Setebos," who sprawls on the shore watching a line of crabs make for the sea, and squashes the twentieth for mere variety and sport. If Jehovah is requested to explain his loves and hates, he answers with Shylock, "it is my whim." It was his whim to love Jacob and hate Esau, and it was no doubt his whim to accept Abel's offering and reject Cain's.

Mythologically the acceptance of Abel's offering and the rejection of Cain's are easily intelligible. The principle of sacrifice was deeply imbedded in Judaism. Without shedding of blood there could be no remission of sin. Under the Levitical law the duties of the priesthood chiefly consisted in burning the sin offerings of the people. It is, therefore, not difficult to understand how the Jewish scribes who wrote or revised the Pentateuch after the Babylonish captivity should give this coloring to the narrative of Genesis; nor is it hard to conceive that for centuries before that date the popular tradition had already, under priestly direction, taken such a color, so as to give the oldest and deepest sanction to the doctrine of animal sacrifice.

It must also be noticed that Abel, who found favor with God, was "a keeper of sheep," while Cain, whose offering was contemned, was "a tiller of the ground." This accords with the strongest traditional instincts of the Jews. The Persian religion decidedly favors agriculture, which it regards as a kind of divine service. Brahminism and Buddhism countenance it still more decidedly, and even go to the length of absolutely prohibiting the slaughter of animals. The Jews, on the other hand, esteemed the pastoral life as the noblest, and the Hebrew historian very naturally represented it as protected and consecrated by the blessing of Jehovah, while agriculture was declared to have been imposed on man as a punishment. The nomadic origin of the Jews accounts for their antipathy to that pursuit, which survived and manifested itself, long after they settled in Palestine, devoted themselves to the cultivation of the soil, and enacted agrarian laws. They always esteemed agriculturalists as inferior to shepherds; men of superior attainments in their histories and legends rose from pastoral life; and kings kept their flocks. David, the man after God's own heart, and the national hero of the Jews, was a shepherd, and the Lord came to him while he was keeping his father's sheep. Moses was keeping his father-in-law's sheep when God appeared to him in the burning bush at Mount Horeb; Jacob kept his uncle Laban's sheep when he fled from Esau; and Abraham, the father of the faithful, was rich in flocks and herds.

To recur to our story. Abel probably enjoyed the conspicuous mark of divine favors conferred on him. Cain, however, experienced very different feelings. He "was very wroth, and his countenance fell." Whereupon the Lord somewhat facetiously asked him what was the matter. "Why," said he, "art thou wroth? and why is thy countenance fallen? If thou doest well, shalt thou not be accepted? and if thou doest not well, sin lieth at the door." This was all very well, but as a matter of fact Cain's offering had already been rejected, and according to the Bible he had done nothing to deserve such harsh treatment.

The Lord's final words on this occasion read thus in our English Bible: "And unto thee shall be his desire, and thou shalt rule over him." These words are construed as applying to Cain's mastery over Abel, as the elder brother; but they seem quite unmeaning in that connexion; for Abel left no offspring, and the prophecy, if such it were, was never fulfilled. Kalisch throws light on this obscure passage. The Lord, he says, was referring not to Abel but to Cain's secret sin, and the passage should read "And to thee is its desire, but thou shalt rule over it."

Cain then "talked with Abel his brother." Gesenius supposes that he communicated to him the words of God, and treats this as the first step towards a reconciliation. However that may be, we hear nothing more of it, for the very next words relate the murder of the younger brother by the elder. "And it came to pass, when they were in the field, that Cain rose up against Abel his brother, and slew him."

This abrupt narrative certainly requires explanation. Kalisch seems to think that Cain went about his work, after the interview with God, in a better frame of mind; but while he toiled hard "in the field" he became incensed at the sight of Abel loafing under a fine umbrageous tree and calmly watching his flock. Forgetting the divine admonitions, and listening only to the voice of passion, he madly killed his only brother, and made himself the first murderer. The Talmud gives several legends about the hatred between the two brothers. One imputes the difference to Cain's avarice, another to his ambition, another to his innate sinfulness, and another to his envy and jealousy on account of Abel's wife. The last of all seems the truest; namely, that they differed "in their views regarding Providence, the moral government of the world, and the efficacy of virtuous deeds for happiness." This idea informs Byron's tragedy on the subject. In "Cain" the younger brother's offering is burnt up with supernatural fire, while the elder's altar remains unkindled; whereupon Cain inveighs against God's partiality, and denounces the bloody sacrifice which finds greater favor than his own peaceful tribute of fruit and flowers. He then advances to scatter the relics of Abel's offering from the altar, but is thwarted by his brother who resists the sacrilege. Abel is felled in the struggle, and Cain, who had no intention of killing him, finds himself an actual murderer before his brother's corpse.

We are bound to conclude that the first quarrel in the world, like nine-tenths of those that have occurred since, was about religion. Cain thought God should be worshiped in one way, Abel thought he should be worshiped in another; and they settled the question, after the manner of religious disputants in all ages, by the stronger knocking the weaker on the head. In religion there is no certitude on this side of the grave; if we are ever destined to know the truth on that subject, we must die to find it out. We may therefore argue fruitlessly until the day of judgment. The only effectual way of settling a religious problem is to settle your opponents.

After the murder the Lord paid Cain another visit, and asked him where Abel was. Cain replied that he was not his brother's keeper and didn't know. He does not appear to have thought God a particularly well informed person. Then the Lord said that Abel's blood cried unto him from the ground. "And now," he continued, "art thou cursed from the earth, which hath opened her mouth to receive thy brother's blood from thy hand; when thou tillest the ground, it shall not henceforth yield unto thee her strength; a fugitive and a vagabond shalt thou be on the earth. And Cain said unto the Lord, my punishment is greater than I can bear. Behold, thou hast driven me out this day from the face of the earth; and from thy face shall I be hid, and I shall be a fugitive and a vagabond in the earth; and it shall come to pass that every one that findeth me shall slay me. And the Lord said unto him, Therefore whosoever slayeth Cain, vengeance shall be taken on him sevenfold. And the Lord set a mark on Cain, lest any finding him should kill him. And Cain went out from the presence of the Lord, and dwelt in the land of Nod, on the east of Eden."

Now let us examine this story. Why was Cain so solicitous about his safety? Why did he fear that everybody would try to kill him? He had slain his brother, and his father and mother were the only people in the world besides himself and perhaps his sisters (? who knew). Kalisch suggests that he apprehended the future vengeance of mankind when the world grew more populous. But how, in that case, could a distinctive mark be any protection? It would publish his identity to all beholders. Besides, one would suppose that Cain, the first man ever born into the world, would always be well known without carrying about a brand like a special wine or a patent edible. And what was the mark? Kalisch thinks it was only a villainous expression. Others think it was the Mongolian type impressed upon the features of Cain, who became the founder of that great division of the human race. A negro preacher started a different theory. When the Lord called out in a loud voice "Cain, where is thy brother Abel," Cain, who was a black man, like Adam, turned pale with fear, and never regained his original color. All his children were pale too; and that, said the preacher, "accounts for de white trash you see ebery war in dese days."

How did Cain manage to go "out from the presence of the Lord," who is everywhere? Satan does the same thing in the Book of Job, and Jonah tries to do it later on. Jehovah was clearly a local as well as a visible God, and not the infinite spirit of the universe.

Where was the land of Nod situated? East of Eden, says the Bible. But nobody knows where Eden was. As we pointed out in "The Creation Story," scores of different positions have been assigned to it. The only point of agreement among the commentators is that it was somewhere. All that can safely be affirmed, then, is that Nod was east of Somewhere. The name itself is very appropriate. No doubt the Lord was not quite awake in that locality, and hence we may explain how Cain managed to go "out from his presence."

In this strange land of Nod, Cain "knew his wife." Who was she? Probably his own sister, but the Bible does not tell us anything about her. Their first son was called Enoch. Cain then "builded a city, and called the name of the city, after the name of his son, Enoch." But this is directly opposed to the curse "a fugitive and a vagabond shalt thou be in the earth."

Delitzsch notices this, and, as usual, seeks to explain it away. Cain, he says, "in this way set himself against the divine curse, in order to feel it inwardly so much the more, as outwardly he seems to have overcome it." To which we reply—first, that there is no evidence that Cain felt the curse "more inwardly" after he built the city; and, secondly, the idea of a man successfully setting himself against an omnipotent curse is a trifle too absurd for credence or criticism.

Now Adam and Eve, when Cain fled after the murder of Abel, were left childless, or at least without a son. But it was necessary that they should have another, in order that God's chosen people, the Jews, might be derived from a purer stock than Cain's. Accordingly we read that Adam, in his hundred and thirtieth year, "begat a son in his own likeness, after his image, and called his name Seth." Why was not Cain begotten in the same way? Had he been so, the cradle of the world might not have been defiled with the blood of fratricide. Seth being "the image" of Adam, and Adam "the image" of God, Seth and the Almighty were of course very much alike. He was pious, and from him were descended the pious patriarchs, including Noah, from whom was descended Abraham the founder of the Jewish race. God's chosen people came of a good stock, although they turned out such a bad lot.

From Seth to Noah there are ten Patriarchs before the Flood. This is clearly mythological. The Hindus believed in ten great saints, the offspring of Manu, and in ten different personifications of Vishnu. The Egyptians had ten mighty heroes, the Chaldeans ten kings before the Flood, the Assyrians ten kings from Ham to Ninyas, and as many from Japhet to Aram; and Plato enumerates ten sons of Neptune, as the rulers of his imaginary Island of Atlantis, submerged by the Deluge.

Cain's descendants were of course drowned by the Flood, but they did a great deal more for the world than the descendants of pious Seth, who seems to have done little else than trust in God. The Cainites laid the basis of civilisation. One of them Jabal, founded cattle-keeping; his brother, Jubal, invented musical instruments; and their half-brother Tubal-cain first practised smithery. Seth's descendants had nothing but piety. Even their morals were no better than those of the Cainites; for at the Flood only eight of them were found worthy of preservations, and they were a poor lot. Noah got beastly drunk after the waters subsided, and one of his three sons brought a curse on all his offspring. What then must we think of the rest?

Tuch excellently explains the mythological significance of the story of Cain and Abel and Seth. "There lies," he says, "in this myth the perfectly correct reminiscence, that in the East ancient nations lived, under whom in very early times culture and civilisation extended, but at the same time the assertion, that these could not prejudice the renown of the Western-Asiatics, since the prerogatives, which their descent from the first-born would secure to them, were done away through God's Curse, which lighted on their ancestor, Cain. Thus the East is cut off from the following history, and the thread fastened on, which carries us on in Genesis, right across through the nations, to the only chosen people of Israel." The entire history of the world before the Flood is dismissed in five chapters, and that from the Flood to Abraham in two more. After that the mighty antique civilisations are never noticed except so far as they affect the history of the Jews. The ages of the Patriarchs also dwindle down from nine centuries in the beginning to almost the normal longevity in the semi-historical period. Could anything more conclusively prove the mythical character of the narrative?

One of the Patriarchs descended from Seth, namely Enoch, which singularly enough is also the name of Cain's eldest son, never died. We read that "he was not, for God took him." It is about time that the Lord took the whole lot out of his Word, and gave us a little ancient history instead. We want a revised Bible in the fullest sense of the word. The old book needs to be completely rewritten. How thankful we should all be if the Lord inspired another "Moses" to rectify the errors and supplement the deficiencies of the first, and to give us scientific truth instead of fanciful myths about the early history of our race! But the Lord never inspires anybody to do a useful piece of work, and our Darwins will therefore have to go on with their slow and laborious task of making out a history of mankind from the multitudinous and scattered traces that still survive the decay of time.

LOT'S WIFE

Lot and his family were a queer lot. Their history is one of the strangest in the whole Bible. They dwelt amongst a people whose debauchery has become a by-word, and in a city which has given a name to the vilest of unnatural crimes. Lot, his wife, and their two unmarried daughters, were the only persons preserved from the terrible fate which Jehovah, in one of his periodic fits of anger, inflicted upon the famous Cities of the Plain. They witnessed a signal instance of his ancient method of dealing with his disobedient children. In the New Testament, God promises the wicked and the unbelievers everlasting fire after they are dead; in the Old Testament, he drowns them or burns them up in this world. Lot and his family saw the destruction of Sodom and Gomorrah by "brimstone and fire from the Lord out of heaven"; and they, four persons in all, just half the number that survived the Flood a few centuries before, were the only ones that escaped. God specially spared them. Yet Lot's wife was turned into a pillar of salt for looking back as she fled from the doomed city, and the old man himself soon after got drunk and committed incest with his daughters. From this crime sprang Moab and Ammon, the founders of two nations who became for many centuries the most implacable enemies of God's chosen people.

Why did the Lord spare these four persons? Why did he not profit by the lesson of the Flood? The eight persons rescued from drowning in that great catastrophe were infected with original sin, and the consequence was that the world peopled from their stock was a great deal worse than the ante-diluvian world. It would clearly have been better to destroy all and start absolutely afresh. The eight rescued persons were apparently just as bad as those who were drowned. So with the four persons spared at the destruction of Sodom. The people of that city could hardly have been much worse than Lot and his children. The Lord appears to have been as stupid in his mercy as he was brutal in his wrath.

Lot was Abraham's nephew, and evidently came of a bad stock. The uncle's evil career will be sketched in our series of "Bible Heroes." For the present we content ourselves with the remark that no good could reasonably be expected from such a family. Lot's father was Haran, a son of Terah, and brother to Abraham.

He "died before his father Terah in the land of his nativity, in Ur of the Chaldees." A city was called by his name in the land of Canaan, and Terah and the family dwelt there after they left Ur, until the patriarch died and Abraham was called out from his kindred to found a new house. The "father of the faithful" took his orphaned nephew with him. Lot accompanied his uncle on the journey to Egypt, where Abraham passed his wife off as his sister, and showed his natural bent by lying right and left.

Soon afterwards we learn that Abraham and Lot had grown very rich, the former "in cattle, in silver, and in gold," and the latter in "flocks, and herds, and tents." Indeed "their substance was so great that they could not dwell together, and there was strife between the herdmen of Abram's cattle and the herd-men of Lot's cattle." Whereupon Abraham said "Don't let us quarrel within the family, but let us part. You can go where you like. If you go to the right I'll go to the left, and if you go to the left I'll go to the right" It was necessary to separate Lot from the fortunes of Abraham, in order that God's dealings with the latter might be uninterrupted and his family kept distinct; and so the Hebrew chronicler very naturally separates them here, in a manner which reflects great credit on Abraham, and exhibits him in a most amiable light.

Cunning Lot took full advantage of the offer. He "lifted up his eyes, and beheld all the plain of Jordan, that it was well watered everywhere, even as the garden of the Lord." So they parted, and Lot "pitched his tent towards Sodom," whose inhabitants, says our naive story, "were wicked and sinners before the Lord exceedingly."

Commentators explain that Lot's approach to such a detestable sink of iniquity indicated the native corruption of his heart, or at least a sad lack of horror at the sins which made the place stink in the nostrils of God.

In the next chapter we find Lot living in Sodom, although we are not told when he moved there. Amraphel king of Shinar, Arioch king of Ellasar, Chedorlaorner king of Elam, and Tidal "king of nations," made war with Bera king of Sodom, Birsha king of Gomorrah, Shinab king of Admah, Shemeber king of Zeboiim, and the "king of Bera, which is Zoar." A great battle was fought in the vale of Siddim, which is alleged to be now covered by the Dead Sea. The four kings were victorious over the five. The kings of Sodom and Gomorrah fled, and the victors spoiled their cities, taking with them many captives, among whom was "Lot, Abram's brother's son." How Abraham went out with a handful of men, defeated the triumphant forces of the allied kings, and rescued his nephew, is a pretty little story which we reserve for our life of that patriarch. All the other captives were rescued also, and Lot, returning with his friends, continued to dwell in Sodom as before.

We hear no more of him for a considerable time. During the interval Abraham has a child by Hagar. Ishmael, with the rest of the patriarch's household, is circumcised. And finally the Lord visits Abraham again to tell him that, notwithstanding their advanced ages, he and Sarah shall yet have a son. What happened during the interview properly belongs to the life of Abraham, but we shall here consider so much of it as relates to the fortunes of Lot.

The Lord complained that the sin of Sodom and Gomorrah was "very grievous," and said that the great cry of it had reached him in heaven. Being much concerned about their "goings on," he had resolved to drop down and see for himself if they were realty as bad as he suspected. "If not," said he, "I will know." In the Old Testament, God, who knows everything, is always seeking information.

Abraham surmised that the Lord meant to play the devil with the Sodomites, and he was anxious about Lot who dwelt with them. So he began a parley. "Now, my Lord," said Abraham, "you surely don't mean to destroy indiscriminately; you, the judge of all the earth, must act on the square. Suppose there are fifty righteous men in Sodom, won't you, just for their sake, spare the place?" Knowing that there were nothing like fifty righteous men in Sodom, the Lord promptly acceded to Abraham's request; so promptly indeed that Abraham smelt a rat, and determined to drive a closer bargain. So he asked the Lord to knock off five. "Very well," was the reply, "if I find forty-five righteous men I'll spare the city." Abraham was still suspicious. He knew that Jehovah loved a bit of destruction, and was not easily moved when he had once made up his mind to indulge himself. So he returned to the charge. "I beg pardon," said he, "for troubling you so, but do you mind knocking off another ten, and making thirty of it?" "Not at all," answered the Lord, "we'll say thirty." Abraham felt there was something wrong. This amiable readiness to oblige thoroughly perplexed him. If the Lord had haggled over the thirty, he would have known that there was about that number of righteous men in the place; but in the actual condition of affairs, he felt that he had considerably overshot the mark. The game was very dangerous, but he decided to renew it. "My Lord," he began, "I'm a dreadful bore, but I'm not quite satisfied with our contract and should like to re-open it. I don't wish to be importunate, but will you knock off another ten?" "With all my heart," replied the Lord, "we'll say twenty." Still dissatisfied, Abraham resolved on a final effort. "My good Lord," said he, "this is really the last time of asking. I promise to bother you no more. Will you knock off another ten?" "All right," was the reply, "anything to oblige. Well say ten altogether. If there are so many righteous men in Sodom I'll spare it. Good afternoon, Abraham, good afternoon." And the Lord was off. Abraham ruefully watched the retreating figure, perfectly assured that the Lord had got the best of the bargain, and that he himself had been duped, worsted, and befooled.

God did not go to Sodom himself, but sent two angels to inspect it. They reached its gate in the evening, and found Lot sitting there. In eastern towns the places before the gate are the appointed localities for meetings; and in ancient times they were used for still more extensive purposes. There the judge pronounced his decisions, and even kings held there occasionally their courts of justice; there buying and selling went on; the people assembled there to see each other and hear the news; and almost all public affairs were transacted there, from religious worship to the smallest details of civil life. It is not surprising, therefore, that Lot should be sitting in the gate when the two strangers arrived at the city. Some commentators have even conjectured that he went out to meet them; but others object that this is contradictory to the narrative, which does not exhibit Lot as recognising the angels, and that it implies "too ideal a notion of its virtue." Some have supposed that Lot had attained to the dignity of a judge, and that he was sitting to act in that capacity on this occasion; but later circumstances refute this supposition; for, in the quarrel which ensued, the people of Sodom reproached him as "a stranger" who set himself up as a judge of their conduct.

Lot advanced to the strangers, greeted them with a profound bow, addressed them as "my lords," and asked them to stay over night at his house, where he would wash their feet, give them something to eat, and find them a bed. They declined his frank hospitality, and said they meant to pass the night in the streets. Kalisch observes, as though he knew all about their motives, that "it was their intention to try his character, and to give him an opportunity of showing whether his generosity was merely a momentary emotion, or had become a settled feature in his character." He also dismisses the idea that they wished to remain in the streets in order to study "the moral state of the Sodomites," as they required no such knowledge, for "they were not only the angels of God, but God himself acted in them." But Kalisch should bear in mind that God told Abraham he was going on purpose to "see whether they have done altogether according to the cry of it"; and that, as the angels could not know more than God, it was after all necessary that they should make inquiries. Lot, however, "pressed upon them greatly," and at last they entered his house. He then "made them a feast" which seems to have consisted of nothing but unleavened bread. Perhaps the angels, who had dined heavily with Abraham on veal, butter, and milk, were afraid of bad dreams, and only wanted a light supper before going to roost.

They were not, however, destined to enjoy a good night's sleep. Before they "lay down," the men of Sodom "compassed the house round, both old and young, all the people from every quarter." And they called unto Lot, and said unto him, "Where are the men which came in unto thee this night? Bring them out unto us, that we may know them."

We are reluctant to criticise this dirty story, but duty compels us. God's Word is full of disgusting narratives, and if we scrupled to examine them we should have to leave the book alone. We have no love of filth, and if the Bible were not held up as a divine work we should never condescend to notice its beastly tales of fornication, adultery, sodomy, and incest.

Why did all the men of Sodom, both old and young, flock to Lot's house? Is it likely that every male in the city, past the age of puberty, should burn with unnatural lust at one and the same time? Did they suppose that all of them could abuse the two strangers? The story is as silly as it is nasty.

For a parallel to Lot's answer to the demand of his neighbors we must go to the nineteenth chapter of Judges, where the men of Gibeah clamor for the Levite as the men of Sodom clamor for the two angels, and where his host offers them instead his own daughter as well as the Levite's concubine. A woman's honor was a very trivial thing to God's chosen people. In itself it counted as next to nothing. The man's right of possession gave it all its importance and worth.

Lot went out and shut the door after him. Then he rebuked his neighbors for desiring to do "so wickedly," and immediately made them an offer which he seems to have thought perfectly fair and square. "Behold, now," he said, "I have two daughters which have not known man; let me, I pray you, bring them out unto you, and do ye to them as is good in your eyes: only unto these men do nothing; for therefore came they under the shadow of my roof." The laws of hospitality are sacred, and Lot did well to maintain them; but he had no right to sacrifice to them a still more sacred law. Instead of strenuously opposing the committal of one crime, he proposes another as heinous.

The Sodomites scorned his offer. They had a penchant for a different pleasure. Ravishing virgins was not in their line. So they reviled Lot for setting himself up as a judge amongst them, called him "fellow," threatened to deal worse with him than with the strangers, and actually pressed so sore upon him that they "came near to break the door."

Then the strangers manifested their power. They "put forth their hand, and pulled Lot into the house to them, and shut too the door. And they smote the men that were at the door of the house with blindness, both small and great; so that they wearied themselves to find the door." However blind they were surely they might have found the door by feeling for it. Kalisch makes this episode more reasonable by substituting "blind confusion" for "blindness."

The angels continued to act promptly. They informed Lot that they intended to destroy the place because of its sin, and told him to gather all his family together and leave at once. Lot spoke to his "sons-in-law, which married his daughters," but they appear to have thought him daft. Early in the morning "the angels hastened Lot" who still lingered. They laid hold of his hand, his wife's, and his two unmarried daughters', led them outside the city, and said, "Escape now for thy life; look not behind thee, neither stay thou in all the plain; escape to the mountains lest thou be consumed." Lot did not relish this prospect of a hard climb. He therefore asked the angels to let him flee unto the city of Zoar, because it was near and "a little one." That is what the servant girl said to her mistress when she produced an illegitimate child, "please 'm its only a very little one." She thought that a small illegitimate baby wasn't as bad as a big illegitimate baby, and Lot thought that a little wicked city wasn't as bad as a big wicked city.

Lot's request was granted, and he was told to look sharp. He made good speed, and reached Zoar when "the sun was risen."

"Then the Lord rained upon Sodom and upon Gomorrah brimstone and fire from the Lord out of heaven; and he overthrew those cities, and all the plain, and all the inhabitants of the cities, and that which grew upon the ground." It is a mistake to suppose that brimstone and fire are characteristic of hell, for the Lord evidently keeps a large stock of those commodities in heaven. Nor must it be supposed that Lot was spared because he was righteous. He was spared because the Lord "was merciful unto him." His virtues, Kalisch remarks, were not sufficient for his salvation, which he owed to "the piety of Abraham." Abraham may have had "piety" enough to save a Lot, but he had scarcely "virtue" enough to save a mouse.

Kalisch says that "about the situation of Zoar there remains little doubt." He identifies it with "the considerable ruins found in Wady Kerek, on the eastern side of the Dead Sea." But he has no such assurance as to the situation of Sodom. He deprecates De Saulcy's assumption, that Sodom is traceable in the heap of stones found near the Salt Mountain, Udsum; and adds—"We may hope rather than expect, that authentic ruins of the four destroyed towns will ever be discovered. Biblical historians and prophets already speak of them as localities utterly and tracelessly swept away; and the remark of Josephus, that 'shadows' of them still existed in his time, is vague and doubtful."

In the South of Palestine there is an extraordinary lake of mysterious origin. It is about thirty-nine miles long, and from eight to twelve miles broad. It is fed by the river Jordan, and drained by the evaporation of a fierce and terrible sun. Its water is clear and inodorous, but nauseous like a solution of alum; it causes painful itching and even ulceration on the lips and if brought near a wound, or any diseased part, produces a most excruciating sensation. It contains muriatic and sulphuric acid, and one-fourth of its weight is salt. No fishes live in it; and according to tradition, which however is not true, birds that happen to fly over its surface die. Near it is said to grow the Apple of Sodom, beautiful in appearance, but containing only ashes. This lake is appropriately called the Dead Sea.

The natives say that at low water they glimpse fragments of buildings and pillars rising out of the bottom of the lake. But this is only a fancy. Yet beneath the waters of the Dead Sea are thought to lie the Cities of the Plain. The northern part of the lake is very deep, the southern part very shallow. The bottom consists of two separate plains, one elevated, the other depressed. The latter is by some held to be the original bottom of the lake, and the former to have been caused by the destruction of Sodom and Gomorrah. But this also is only a fancy. The bitumen, which is found in such large quantities in and near the lake, is a symptom and remnant of the volcanic nature of the region. Several lines of earthquake are traced from it in a north-eastern direction; and it is conjectured that the three lakes, Merom, Tiberias, and Asphaltites, together with the river Jordan, are the remaining traces of the huge gulf once filled by the Dead Sea before the land was lifted by a geological catastrophe. Volcanic action has caused all the remarkable phenomena of the district, which were of immemorial antiquity thousands of years ago; and the story of the Cities of the Plain is only one of the legends which ancient peoples associated with every striking aspect of nature.

Let us recur to Lot. His sons, his married daughters, and their husbands, perished in the deluge of brimstone and fire. He and his two unmarried daughters fled to Zoar as fast as their legs could carry them. But his wife was less fortunate. She ran behind Lot, and with the natural curiosity of her sex she looked back on the doomed city. For this violation of the angels' orders she was turned into "a pillar of salt." Some commentators try to blink this unpleasant fact by artful translations; such as "she fell into a salt-brook," or "she was covered with a salt crust," or she was "like a pillar of salt." Josephus pretended to have seen this old woman of salt, but others have been less lucky, although many travellers and pilgrims have searched for it as for a sacred relic. But let us not despair. Lot's wife may yet be discovered and exhibited in the British Museum.

What became of Lot and his daughters? Fearing to dwell in Zoar, they left it and "dwelt in a cave." The damsels, who had heard their father offer them to the promiscuous embrace of a lustful crowd, could not be expected to be very scrupulous in their conduct. They were alone, without husbands to make them mothers, and to be childless was a calamity and a reproach; so they put their heads together and devised a nasty scheme. Two nights successively they made their father blind drunk, and got him to commit incest with them. This is very beastly and very absurd. Lot was old; he was so drunk that he knew nothing of what happened; yet he got two virgins with child! The porter in "Macbeth" would have laughed at such a ridiculous story.

These improper females were by no means ashamed of their action; on the contrary, they boast of their bastards; and the historian does not utter a word in condemnation of their crime.

Lot was the father of his own grandchildren; his daughters were the mothers of their own brothers; and his other children were destroyed by heavenly brimstone and fire. Were they not, as we said at the outset, a queer lot? But the queerest lot was Lot's wife. Whatever may be said of the rest of the family, no one can say that she was not worth her salt, for the Lord thought she was worth enough to make a pillar. Let us hope that the old lady will some day be (un)covered, and that her pillar of salt may yet, to the confusion of sceptics, stand as a veritable pillar in the house of God, and there defy the attacks of all the infidel Samsons, world without end. Amen.

www.ingramcontent.com/pod-product-compliance
Lightning Source LLC
Chambersburg PA
CBHW011255040426
42453CB00015B/2419